Dreams that Heal and Counsel

Hearing God's voice in the night

Dreams that Heal and Counsel

© 2004 Steve and Dianne Bydeley

All rights reserved. No part of this publication may be reproduced, stored in a retrieval system, or transmitted in any form or by any means-electronic, mechanical, photocopy, recording, or any other-except for brief quotations in printed reviews, without the prior written permission of the authors.

Unless otherwise noted, Scripture quotations taken from the New American Standard Bible®, Copyright © 1960, 1962, 1963, 1968, 1971, 1972, 1973, 1975, 1977, 1995 by The Lockman Foundation. Used by permission. (www.Lockman.org)

Scripture quotations marked NIV are taken from the HOLY BIBLE, NEW INTERNATIONAL VERSION®, NIV®. Copyright © 1973, 1978, 1984, by International Bible Society. Used by permission of Zondervan Publishing House. All rights reserved.

Scripture quotations marked "NKJV™" are taken from the New King James Version®. Copyright © 1982 by Thomas Nelson, Inc. Used by permission. All rights reserved.

Scripture quotations marked NLT are taken from the Holy Bible, New Living Translation, copyright © 1996. Used by permission of Tyndale House Publishers, Inc., Wheaton, Illinois 60189 by Tyndale Charitable Trust. All rights reserved.

ISBN: 0-9731458-8-9

Lapstone Publications
Kitchener, Ontario
E-mail: info@lapstoneministries.org
Website: www.lapstoneministries.org
Printed in Canada

"The "Wonder of a Counselor" communicates with His loved ones, not through the preferred Western approach of logic, but through dreams, visions, and symbols.

"Steve and Dianne draw on their rich and varied backgrounds to illustrate how God communicates His love and healing through a variety of angles, and make specific application from Biblical texts about dreams and visions.

"This book stimulates ones' thinking about the wealth of information that is in scriptures and how God wants to bring healing to the world."

Rev. Arthur Zeilstra, Director,
Cornerstone Christian Counselling Centre,
Waterloo, Ontario, Canada

"While reading *Dreams that Heal and Counsel*, I was mightily blessed and experienced further healing and release because the Holy Spirit backs the truth expounded in this book.

"Dreams are most often for and about the dreamer and one of the ways God communicates with his children involves a personal code—the dream language. Learning that the imagery is a personal code from a personal God has helped me understand more of my past dreams. Since reading this book I have been dreaming more. I now enjoy better communication with God as together we interpret my dreams."

David Durnan,
Home Group Leader
Toronto Airport Christian Fellowship

"*Dreams that Heal and Counsel* is a warm, user friendly book on the topic of hearing from God through your dreams. Steve and Dianne write with authority and yet simplicity as they take you through the many dreams of the Bible, showing you the vast assortment of healing, direction and counsel which God gives us through dreams at night. This book is full of many dreams from today and provides clear simple instructions as to how to interpret them and be enlightened by them. I recommend this book to all. You will come away refreshed."

Dr. Mark Virkler
Communion With God Ministries
President of Christian Leadership University

We dedicate this book to those in the body of Christ who are searching for a closer relationship with God.

Our thanks and appreciation goes to the many friends who have contributed, helped prepare the manuscript, offered direction, and given encouragement including Rev. Arthur and Chris Zeilstra, David and Karen Durnan...

Most of all we are thankful, with our whole being, to the giver of dreams-God our Savior, Jesus.

Outline

...DEDICATION	iii
...OUTLINE	v
... FOREWORD	xi
...PREFACE	xiii
1...I WILL SPEAK TO THEM	1
WHY SO DIFFICULT?	5
2...DREAMS - PENTATEUCH	9
ABIMELECH'S PLIGHT	10
JACOB'S STORY	11
No sweet Talk	11
THE JOSEPH STORY	12
Prison Ministry	13
Famine to Feast	15
Feast and Famine	16
Reunion	17
IDENTIFYING A PROPHET	19
DISCERNING PROPHETS	19
3...DREAMS - JUDGES TO PROPHETS	21
GIDEON'S ENCOURAGEMENT	21
SAUL'S DISTRESS	22
SOLOMON'S PROMISE	23
ELIHU'S COUNSEL	25
COUNSEL TO FALSE PROPHETS	26
THE HEART OF THE KING	27
Driven to Repentance	29
FUTURE EVENTS	33

THE OUTPOURING	36
TELLING FALSE DREAMS	36
4...DREAMS - NEW TESTAMENT	37
BIRTH OF JESUS	37
CHURCH GROWTH	39
MISSIONS VENTURE	41
REVELATION	41
CONCLUSION	41
5...A PRIMER ON DREAM TYPES	43
DREAM CATEGORIES	45
TYPES OF MESSAGE DREAMS	45
CONCLUSION	47
6...SYMBOLS IN DREAMS - A PRIMER	49
PERSONAL DREAMS	49
IMPERSONAL OR INTERPERSONAL DREAMS	50
Impersonal Dreams	50
Interpersonal Dreams	51
Responding to These Dreams	51
DREAM SYMBOLS IN PERSONAL DREAMS	52
LEFT/RIGHT BRAIN ACTIVITIES	54
LITERAL DREAMS	56
RECORDING YOUR DREAMS	57
CONCLUSION	57
7...COUNSELED IN THE NIGHT	59
Black Dog	59
COUNSEL	60
Supported Walk	60
Leaving	61
Relationships	62
Mechanical Monster	63
No Backing Up	63
Crime Scene	64
Download	65
Comfort	67
Guidance	68
Eagle's Flight	69
Waiting Rooms	71
Missed the Plane	72
CONCLUSIONS	72

Outline

8...SANCTIFICATION	75
THE PROCESS OF SANCTIFICATION	76
Rooted in the Garden	77
Our Spirit	78
Our Soul	79
Our Body	80
THE WORK OF THE CROSS	80
CONCLUSION	81
9...INNER HEALING	83
Marked at Birth	85
DEFINITION	86
TRIGGERING A ROOT MEMORY	87
Golf	89
Scolding	91
Roots	91
Rejection	92
MEMORIES AND DISSOCIATION	94
CONCLUSION	95
10...HEALING DREAM SYMBOLS	97
PEOPLE VERSUS ROLES	97
RELATIVES IN DREAMS	99
Fathers	99
Mothers	101
Children	101
New Born Dream	102
THE DREAMER'S CHILDREN	103
No Diapers Dream	103
Coffin Dream	103
Piano Dream	104
Grandparents	104
Tractor Dream	106
BUILDINGS OR ROOMS	106
Childhood Roots	108
The Shed	108
CLOSETS, BASEMENTS, AND ATTICS	108
The Way of the Closet	109
Wet Floor	109
TOILETS, BATHS, AND SHOWERS	110
Busy Washroom	110

ACTIONS IN DREAMS	111
SEXUAL DREAMS	113
Cheating Dream	113
Intimate Qualities Dream	114
Nakedness in Dreams	114
CONCLUSION	114
11...DREAMS AND INNER HEALING	117
HEALING DREAMS	118
TV Programming	118
The Frog	119
The Bathroom Stall	120
School Yard	121
The Operation	122
The Racetrack	123
Swimming the River	124
Snake's Tongue	125
Mother in the River	125
Green Park	126
Wrong Steps	127
Clark Gable	128
French Décor	128
Hospital Baby	129
African Savannah	130
Secondhand Auction	131
Mountain Desert	132
CONCLUSION	133
12...THE DREAMS OF CHILDREN	135
THE CAREGIVER'S DREAM	136
Daycare Dilemma	136
Bloody Mary	137
The Mud Girl	138
Snakes	139
Ice Cream	139
CONCLUSION	139
13...RESPONDING TO DREAMS	141
OUR OWN DREAMS	142
When We Need Help	143
THE DREAMS OF OTHERS	144
14...CONCLUSIONS	147

Outline

... ENDNOTES 151
... BIBLIOGRAPHY 155
…ABOUT THE AUTHORS 157

x

Foreword

Most of us have read books on healing. Some of us have read books on dreams. But how many of us have ever read an author who has been able to put these two topics together? Enjoy the fresh and timely insights that the Bydeleys share in this new book. You will be challenged and want to experience more as you read through their penetrating chapters. We challenge you.

Chester and Betsy Kylstra
Healing House Ministries International,
International Healing Center, Henderson, NC
Authors of Restoring the Foundation, and
An Integrated Approach to Biblical Healing Ministry

Preface

We have written Dreams that Heal and Counsel as a sequel to Dream Dreams. As you would expect, since then we have continued to explore and learn about the many ways in which God uses dreams to speak, teach, and guide us. If you have not already read Dream Dreams, you may want to consider doing so, as it devotes much more time to the process and details of dream interpretation. We see it as foundational to understanding dreams.

This new offering represents our findings. Among other things, we look specifically at how our Father uses dreams to influence his goal—sanctification—in our lives. This results in greater intimacy with him and with others.

God saves us into the body of Christ—into relationship and a need for each other. He gives some of his truth to different members of the body of believers to encourage our need for each other. No one member has all the truth. No one denomination has all the truth. No individual, regardless of the anointing he or she carries, has all the truth. If we want more of God's truth, we must be in relationship with the members of his body. With this in mind, we affirm that we do not understand everything there is to know concerning dreams. God has entrusted us with some truth on the subject, just as he has with other believers. We encourage you to read what other Christians are discovering about the nature of dreams.

Dianne and I are pastoral counselors who specialize in inner healing and deliverance as they relate to personal and relationship problems and physical healing. Through our search for insights, we are learning how wonderfully God uses dreams to minister in these areas of our lives. We view it as a manifestation of his love and desire to be in fellowship with us. We are also discovering how God, our Father, is even bigger than we imagined. His love and creativity is measureless, beyond the confines that we so often impose on him.

May God bless and guide you as you pursue a greater understanding of dreams, their message, and his love and healing in your life.

1 I Will Speak to Them

Hear now My words: If there is a prophet among you, I, the LORD, shall make Myself known to him in a vision. I shall speak with him in a dream (Numbers 12:6).

"In this dream, I learned that a man of stature, wealth, and prominence chose me. There were other beautiful and glamorous women, and yet some people came to my home saying that this man had chosen me. I was shocked; I didn't think I had a chance. I didn't look like those other women and was not as smart as they were. However, the people said they had been watching everyone closely and they chose me because I was beautiful on the inside and had the qualities he sought.

"One of them placed the most beautiful heart-shaped diamond ring on my finger. The center diamond was smoky and around it were four clear diamonds. The ring was very large. The setting of the center diamond was unique; it rose as if on a small spring that allowed the diamond to move. I kept looking at the ring on my finger, unable to believe what was happening.

"I got into a limo and they took me somewhere and prepared me to meet the man. I felt so honored; people everywhere were blessing me. I thought I was dreaming. It was strange; I remembered I was already married to Ron, so I could not marry the man. However, it seemed as if that was not an issue. I was so happy. I felt set apart, special. I knew this was how life should be."

Was this just a dream or was it more—a message perhaps? We are sure that nearly everybody at some time has had a dream that seemed to convey a message. Do these dreams carry a message from God or are they, as some suggest, merely the random neuron activity of a bored brain waiting for the body to wake?

The woman who had this dream recounted that prior to it, she had always felt as if she was a grain of sand lost in a vast desert. She loved the Lord very much and enjoyed spending time with him in prayer and worship, but until she had this dream she felt insignificant. Now she glows.

Reading even a small portion of the Bible reveals that God has spoken to his people in dreams and visions. In the book of Job, considered by many scholars to be one of the earliest books written, we read this about dreams:

> "For God does speak—now one way, now another—though man may not perceive it. In a dream, in a vision of the night, when deep sleep falls on men as they slumber in their beds, he may speak in their ears and terrify them with warnings, to turn man from wrongdoing and keep him from pride, to preserve his soul from the pit, his life from perishing by the sword" (Job 33:14–18 NIV).

The excerpt starts with the words "For God does speak." Do we, when reading this, perceive it to be in the past tense—"God did speak"—believing he no longer does?

In our western culture, many people feel that rational thought and sensory perception are the only means by which we can gain understanding. This is also true among many in the Christian community. At times it seems as if we have become slaves to our senses and to reason, letting them govern what we know, how we feel, and how we live. Yet the Bible tells us that we will find our life by losing it for Jesus' sake,[1] that it is in giving that we receive,[2] and that the meek will inherit the earth.[3] Each of these principles is true, yet a paradox when analyzed by rational thinkers. Knowing that God does not change,[4] which then is reasonable: "God did speak," or "God does speak" through dreams?

The Gospel of Matthew reveals that God spoke through dreams, giving important messages. In the first few chapters, we see several examples:

- ◆Joseph told to take Mary as his wife[5]
- ◆The Magi warned to avoid King Herod[6]
- ◆Joseph told to flee to Egypt[7]
- ◆Joseph told to return to Israel[8]
- ◆Joseph encouraged to settle in Galilee[9]

Each of these dreams and the messages in them were pivotal in protecting the infant Jesus and ensuring God's plan for our salvation.

Of course, how God's people viewed dreams and their messages was a crucial factor also. Joseph obviously believed in their significance enough to obey them, as did Peter when he received an important vision in Acts. Imagine the outcome if Peter had dismissed the merits of dreams or visions[10] when he saw the image of a sheet (better translated as "a sail") full of unclean animals descending from heaven.[11] Would he have followed the Gentiles to their home when they came asking for him? We can only speculate on the alternatives. We do know that on this occasion God spoke through a vision to Peter, who seemed then to be the head of the church, on a matter of immense importance to both Christians and gentiles.

Does God only speak to us through the written words of the Bible? If we believe this is so, then we must acknowledge that within its pages he has spoken in significant ways through dreams and visions. And in those same pages he has promised to do so today. God spoke through the prophet Joel, declaring that in the day of the Lord:

> "It will come about after this That I will pour out My Spirit on all mankind; And your sons and daughters will prophesy, Your old men will dream dreams, Your young men will see visions" (Joel 2:28).

Hundreds of years later, Peter, in his preaching debut on the day of Pentecost,[12] identifies the supernatural events of that day as fulfilling Joel's prophecy. The presence of the Holy Spirit in the lives of his people, then and now, brings prophecy, dreams, and visions. Jesus also confirmed this when he spoke of the Holy Spirit:

> "He will speak; and He will disclose to you what is to come . . . . He will take of Mine and will disclose it to you" (John 16:13–14).

Did all this end with the death of the original Apostles? Chrysostom, Tertullian, Cyprian, Synesius, and other leaders of the post-apostolic church spoke of the significance of dreams to life and ministry of the church.[13]

Perhaps you are reading this book because God has been speaking to you in dreams and visions and you are interested in understanding the messages. Or you may be interested in the prospect that God wants to speak to you through dreams. Consider the woman who had been praying for her ailing mother. In a dream she saw a plane and heard a voice speaking a date. She responded by booking a flight for that date to visit her mother. Her obedience made possible a memorable visit with her mother, who died less than a week later.

"For God does speak" (Job 33:14 NIV).

Why so Difficult?

People often ask us why God seems to make it so difficult for us to discern his message in dreams. Why does he not tell us plainly what he wants of us, so we can respond? We can think of two possible reasons why dreams seem difficult to understand. First, perhaps we have been educated away from the intuitive. Our education system focuses on science and technology more than on the arts and the abstract. Secondly, if God made things easy, would that really be better for us? Is it possible that God knows us better than we know ourselves?

When things are easy for us—when we are told exactly what to do and how to do it—we often do what is required of us, but no more. Not much different from a robot. However, when a task is difficult and we are not quite sure how to accomplish it, we sometimes give more of ourselves and rise to a new level. As we stretch ourselves to meet the challenges of a new endeavor, we often thrive.

Adam was given the responsibility to name all the animals and, with Eve, to care for the earth.[14] God probably did not tell them what they needed to do—that was for them to figure out. He did not create us as robots, to simply do what he tells us. If we were, he could give us orders, tell us exactly how to fulfill the orders, and we would execute those orders—and nothing more. But God made us in his image[15] and gave us the capacity to make choices—to think and to reason. He expects more of us than robots and wants us to use the faculties he has given us.

Paul directed the church in Thessalonica that "if anyone is not willing to work, then he is not to eat, either" (2 Thessalonians 3:10). He understood that we often have little respect for things we do not work for. There is seldom a reward for doing nothing.

We also read from Proverbs that "it is the glory of God to conceal a matter, But the glory of kings is to search out a matter" (25:2). The meaning of the word translated "glory" is rooted in the words "burden or heaviness."[16] When we add that perspective to this verse, we read: "It is God's burden, or perhaps responsibility, to hide a matter, and a king's burden, or job to search it out." God knows we need to work for things in order that we grow into mature children of God. He knows that making things easy for us is often not in our best interest.

Before the children of Israel entered the Promised Land, God could have removed the inhabitants, leaving their homes and farms intact for the Israelites to use. Instead, he promised to go before the Israelites, fighting as they fought. Working with God, the Israelites were strong and prospered.

God speaks to us in a "picture language," using parables, dreams, visions, prophetic utterances, and his word. Our challenge is to discover the often concealed message. It is a process of discovery and it should be an enjoyable one. Staying close to the Father is an important part of it.

Could the life and ministries of our churches and their members benefit from an increased interest and enthusiasm for dreams and visions? Are we missing a significant source of intimacy and relationship with the Father? Does God affect healing through our dreams and visions? These are the questions we hope you will explore with us.

Steve & Dianne Bydeley

2   Dreams – Genesis to Joshua

Does God heal and counsel us through dreams and visions? There is no better place to look for answers than the Bible.

In the next three chapters we take a trip through the scriptures, reading some of the many accounts of how God spoke to his people through dreams and visions. We also offer brief commentaries and possible applications to our lives. Some of the biblical excerpts are lengthy, but we include them in order that you may adapt this study to a format that suits you. In addition to discovering evidence of healing and counseling in dreams, we hope that you will find ways to apply what you learn to your lives—usually the biggest challenge. This study will also yield an increased understanding of God's character. Let's enjoy this time of relationship with God as we explore his word together. Lead on Holy Spirit!

A word of caution before we start. Many of us are tempted to glide over "familiar" portions of scripture looking for something that is a little less familiar. Try to avoid this temptation and read each passage with fresh eyes, free, if possible, of preconceived interpretations.

Abimelech's Plight

In Genesis, we read of the wanderings of Abraham and his beautiful wife Sarah. While staying with Abimelech, the king of Gerar, Abraham became fearful that Abimelech would kill him in order to have Sarah, so he told the king that Sarah was his sister. Abimelech then took her.

> "But God came to Abimelech in a dream of the night, and said to him, 'Behold, you are a dead man because of the woman whom you have taken, for she is married.' Now Abimelech had not come near her; and he said, 'Lord, will You slay a nation, even though blameless? Did he not himself say to me, "She is my sister "? And she herself said, "He is my brother." In the integrity of my heart and the innocence of my hands I have done this.'
>
> "Then God said to him in the dream, 'Yes, I know that in the integrity of your heart you have done this, and I also kept you from sinning against Me; therefore I did not let you touch her. Now therefore, restore the man's wife, for he is a prophet, and he will pray for you and you will live. But if you do not restore her, know that you shall surely die, you and all who are yours.' So Abimelech arose early in the morning and called all his servants and told all these things in their hearing; and the men were greatly frightened" (Genesis 20:3–8).

In this dream, God told Abimelech to return Sarah to Abraham; otherwise he would die. Consider how God entrusted such a life-or-death message to a dream. Abimelech wisely demonstrated his belief in the message by restoring Sarah to Abraham. By heeding the counsel of the dream, he literally saved his life and those of his household.

Jacob's Story

More than 100 years later, God spoke to Abraham's grandson Jacob in a number of dreams. We pick up the story when Jacob has been working as a shepherd for his crooked uncle Laban for several years. He laments to his wives Rachel and Leah, who are Laban's daughters, of Laban's dishonesty, yet he consoles himself that God is with him. He tells of a significant dream to justify his accumulated wealth at their father's expense and the reason for his determination to leave Laban and return to the land of his fathers.

> "And it came about at the time when the flock were mating that I lifted up my eyes and saw in a dream and behold, the male goats which were mating were striped, speckled, and mottled. Then the angel of God said to me in the dream, 'Jacob,' and I said, 'Here I am.' He said, 'Lift up now your eyes and see that all the male goats which are mating are striped, speckled, and mottled; for I have seen all that Laban has been doing to you. I am the God of Bethel, where you anointed a pillar, where you made a vow to Me; now arise, leave this land, and return to the land of your birth'" (Genesis 31:10–13).

This dream is an example of how God offers both comfort and counsel to his people. When Jacob was discouraged at how Laban constantly cheated him, God consoled him. He then gave Jacob counsel, declaring that his exile was over. The time had come for him to leave Laban and return to the land of his birth, the land promised to him through Abraham and Isaac. All of this had great implications for the future of God's people.

No Sweet Talk

The time to depart was at hand. After living and working for Laban for more than 20 years and marrying his two daughters, it was time to leave. But Jacob did not trust Laban to voluntarily let him go, so he secretly fled with his household and all he had acquired. When Laban discovered this he was angry and, together with his relatives, pursued Jacob and caught up with him in the hill country of Gilead. However, before Laban actually confronted Jacob, God spoke to him in a dream in the night saying, "Be careful that you do not speak to Jacob either good or bad" (Genesis 31:24). The next day, Laban confronted Jacob.

> "What have you done by deceiving me and carrying away my daughters like captives of the sword? Why did you flee secretly and deceive me, and did not tell me so that I might have sent you away with joy and with songs, with timbrel and with lyre; and did not allow me to kiss my sons and my daughters? Now you have done foolishly. It is in my power to do you harm, but the God of your father spoke to me last night, saying, 'Be careful not to speak either good or bad to Jacob'" (Genesis 31:26–29).

God's counsel was clear. Laban was not to sweet-talk or threaten Jacob into returning with him. Laban had the means to harm Jacob and might have done so, save for his respect for God's voice and willingness to obey it. Again, without God's direct intervention in a dream, events might have taken a disastrous turn.

The Joseph Story

Jacob, now known as Israel, eventually settled in his birth region of Canaan. Of his 12 sons, he favored the second youngest, Joseph. The other brothers knew this and despised Joseph. And then Joseph started telling his dreams.

> "Joseph had a dream, and when he told it to his brothers, they hated him even more. He said to them, 'Please

listen to this dream which I have had; for behold, we were binding sheaves in the field, and lo, my sheaf rose up and also stood erect; and behold, your sheaves gathered around and bowed down to my sheaf.' Then his brothers said to him, 'Are you actually going to reign over us? Or are you really going to rule over us?' So they hated him even more for his dreams and for his words.

"Now he had still another dream, and related it to his brothers, and said, 'Lo, I have had still another dream; and behold, the sun and the moon and eleven stars were bowing down to me.' He related it to his father and to his brothers; and his father rebuked him and said to him, 'What is this dream that you have had? Shall I and your mother and your brothers actually come to bow ourselves down before you to the ground?' His brothers were jealous of him, but his father kept the saying in mind" (Genesis 37:5–11).

Joseph's brothers hated him—this portion of scripture mentions it twice. Consider what might have happened if the brothers had acknowledged their hatred, repented of it, and allowed the Lord to resolve things.

Through this interpersonal dream, the Lord was trying to counsel the brothers to honor and respect Joseph. Many years later, as his brothers bowed to him, Joseph pondered these dreams, knowing that they were being fulfilled.

Prison Ministry

Joseph's brothers acted on their hatred, secretly selling him into slavery and telling their father that a wild animal had killed him. Joseph ended up in Egypt where he was falsely accused and imprisoned. Among the inmates were two important men—Pharaoh's personal cupbearer and his chief baker. They had both offended the Pharaoh. One night, each of these men had a dream that neither could understand. The next morning, the men confided to Joseph that they had no one to interpret the dreams. Joseph replied that interpretation belongs to God and invited them to tell him their dreams.

"So the chief cupbearer told his dream to Joseph, and said to him, 'In my dream, behold, there was a vine in front of me; and on the vine were three branches. And as it was budding, its blossoms came out, and its clusters produced ripe grapes. Now Pharaoh's cup was in my hand; so I took the grapes and squeezed them into Pharaoh's cup, and I put the cup into Pharaoh's hand.'

"Then Joseph said to him, 'This is the interpretation of it: the three branches are three days; within three more days Pharaoh will lift up your head and restore you to your office; and you will put Pharaoh's cup into his hand according to your former custom when you were his cupbearer.

"'Only keep me in mind when it goes well with you, and please do me a kindness by mentioning me to Pharaoh and get me out of this house. For I was in fact kidnapped from the land of the Hebrews, and even here I have done nothing that they should have put me into the dungeon'" (Genesis 40:9–15).

After hearing this favorable interpretation, the baker was eager to share his dream to see what Joseph's God would reveal to him.

"When the chief baker saw that he had interpreted favorably, he said to Joseph, 'I also saw in my dream, and behold, there were three baskets of white bread on my head; and in the top basket there were some of all sorts of baked food for Pharaoh, and the birds were eating them out of the basket on my head.'

"Then Joseph answered and said, 'This is its interpretation: the three baskets are three days; within three more days Pharaoh will lift up your head from you and will hang you on a tree, and the birds will eat your flesh off you'" (Genesis 40:16–19).

Famine to Feast

The cupbearer was restored to his position in Pharaoh's court, but neglected to mention Joseph's unjust imprisonment. And then Pharaoh started dreaming.

"Now it happened at the end of two full years that Pharaoh had a dream, and behold, he was standing by the Nile. And lo, from the Nile there came up seven cows, sleek and fat; and they grazed in the marsh grass. Then behold, seven other cows came up after them from the Nile, ugly and gaunt, and they stood by the other cows on the bank of the Nile. The ugly and gaunt cows ate up the seven sleek and fat cows.

"Then Pharaoh awoke. He fell asleep and dreamed a second time; and behold, seven ears of grain came up on a single stalk, plump and good. Then behold, seven ears, thin and scorched by the east wind, sprouted up after them. The thin ears swallowed up the seven plump and full ears.

"Then Pharaoh awoke, and behold, it was a dream. Now in the morning his spirit was troubled, so he sent and called for all the magicians of Egypt, and all its wise men. And Pharaoh told them his dreams, but there was no one who could interpret them to Pharaoh" (Genesis 41:1–8).

Two years passed after the cupbearer was released and Joseph was still in prison. Then God spoke to Pharaoh through two dramatic dreams that left him troubled, as he did not understand them. He called for his court magicians and wise men, but no one was able to interpret them.

Feast and Famine

God may then have nudged the memory of the cup-bearer, because he told Pharaoh of his experiences in prison and how a young Hebrew prisoner had correctly interpreted his dream and that of the baker. Perhaps Joseph could be of assistance to Pharaoh.

> "Then Pharaoh sent and called for Joseph, and they hurriedly brought him out of the dungeon; and when he had shaved himself and changed his clothes, he came to Pharaoh. Pharaoh said to Joseph, 'I have had a dream, but no one can interpret it; and I have heard it said about you, that when you hear a dream you can interpret it.' Joseph then answered Pharaoh, saying, 'It is not in me; God will give Pharaoh a favorable answer.'
>
> "So Pharaoh spoke to Joseph, 'In my dream, behold, I was standing on the bank of the Nile; and behold, seven cows, fat and sleek came up out of the Nile, and they grazed in the marsh grass. Lo, seven other cows came up after them, poor and very ugly and gaunt, such as I had never seen for ugliness in all the land of Egypt; and the lean and ugly cows ate up the first seven fat cows. Yet when they had devoured them, it could not be detected that they had devoured them, for they were just as ugly as before.
>
> "'Then I awoke. I saw also in my dream, and behold, seven ears, full and good, came up on a single stalk; and lo, seven ears, withered, thin, and scorched by the east wind, sprouted up after them; and the thin ears swallowed the seven good ears.
>
> "'Then I told it to the magicians, but there was no one who could explain it to me.' Now Joseph said to Pharaoh, 'Pharaoh's dreams are one and the same; God has told to Pharaoh what He is about to do. The seven good cows are seven years; and the seven good ears are

seven years; the dreams are one and the same. The seven lean and ugly cows that came up after them are seven years, and the seven thin ears scorched by the east wind will be seven years of famine.

"'It is as I have spoken to Pharaoh: God has shown to Pharaoh what He is about to do. Behold, seven years of great abundance are coming in all the land of Egypt; and after them seven years of famine will come, and all the abundance will be forgotten in the land of Egypt, and the famine will ravage the land. So the abundance will be unknown in the land because of that subsequent famine; for it will be very severe. Now as for the repeating of the dream to Pharaoh twice, it means that the matter is determined by God, and God will quickly bring it about'" (Genesis 41:14–32).

Joseph quickly recognized that God was repeating the same message in both dreams, and that this repetition underscored the certainty of the dreams being fulfilled. Seven years of famine would follow seven years of plenty. Being forewarned, Pharaoh could prepare for these events. As we shall see he did, and those preparations ensured the survival of not only Egypt, but also of God's people.

Reunion

Pharaoh immediately released Joseph from prison and appointed him governor of all of Egypt, answerable only to Pharaoh. In that position, Joseph managed the years of plenty, owing to skills he learned as a slave.[17] During the seven years of plenty, Joseph stored extra food for the famine that lay ahead. When it finally struck, Egypt had food. People came from the neighboring countries to buy grain, including ten of Joseph's brothers. When they came for an audience with Joseph, he recognized them.

"But Joseph had recognized his brothers, although they

did not recognize him. Joseph remembered the dreams which he had about them, and said to them, 'You are spies; you have come to look at the undefended parts of our land'" (Genesis 42:8–9).

This scripture is included because it has some interesting healing issues. When Joseph recognized his brothers, he remembered the dreams of the sheaves bowing and the stars, the moon, and the sun bowing to him. Here they were, bowing low before him just as the dreams had foreshadowed. He also remembered his brothers' jealousy and their betrayal of him. For whatever reason, he decided to conceal his identity from his brothers and make life difficult for them, so he accused them of being spies.

In the months that followed, Joseph tested his brothers in different ways. Much worried, they remembered their cruel treatment of Joseph.

"Truly we are guilty concerning our brother [Joseph], because we saw the distress of his soul when he pleaded with us, yet we would not listen; therefore this distress has come upon us" (Genesis 42:21).

Eventually, after testing the attitude of the brothers, Joseph reveals his identity to them. At the same time, he admonishes them not to be angry with themselves for their harsh treatment of him years earlier, declaring that it was part of God's plan.

"Then Joseph said to his brothers, 'Please come closer to me.' And they came closer. And he said, 'I am your brother Joseph, whom you sold into Egypt. Now do not be grieved or angry with yourselves, because you sold me here, for God sent me before you to preserve life. For the famine has been in the land these two years, and there are still five years in which there will be neither ploughing nor harvesting.

"'God sent me before you to preserve for you a remnant in the earth, and to keep you alive by a great deliverance. Now, therefore, it was not you who sent me here, but God; and He has made me a father to Pharaoh and lord of all his household and ruler over all the land of Egypt.

"'Hurry and go up to my father, and say to him, "Thus says your son Joseph, God has made me lord of all Egypt; come down to me, do not delay. You shall live in the land of Goshen, and you shall be near me, you and your children and your children's children and your flocks and your herds and all that you have. There I will also provide for you, for there are still five years of famine to come, and you and your household and all that you have would be impoverished"'" (Genesis 45: 4–11).

Joseph was able to forgive his brothers, which allowed healing to come into their relationships. Through the counsel of two dreams a very long time ago, God showed that he was at work in their lives, healing, caring, and protecting.

Identifying a Prophet

"He said, 'Hear now My words: If there is a prophet among you, I, the LORD, shall make Myself known to him in a vision. I shall speak with him in a dream'"(Numbers 12:6).

Does God communicate through dreams? Does he give counsel and bring healing into heart issues? A result of God revealing himself through dreams and visions is that we will receive his counsel and healing.

Discerning Prophets

"If a prophet or a dreamer of dreams arises among you and gives you a sign or a wonder, and the sign or the wonder comes true, concerning which he spoke to you, saying, 'Let us go after other gods (whom you have not known) and let us serve them,' you shall not listen to the words of that prophet or that dreamer of dreams; for the LORD your God is testing you to find out if you love the LORD your God with all your heart and with all your soul" (Deuteronomy 13:1–3).

God sometimes tests us or puts us in situations where we manifest what is really in our hearts, as our hearts motivate our actions. This scripture warns us that some people may proclaim themselves to be prophets and dreamers of dreams, and they may be able to perform signs or wonders, but if we are not careful, they may lead us away from God.

"You shall follow the LORD your God and fear Him; and you shall keep His commandments, listen to His voice, serve Him, and cling to Him. But that prophet or that dreamer of dreams shall be put to death, because he has counseled rebellion against the LORD your God who brought you from the land of Egypt and redeemed you from the house of slavery, to seduce you from the way in which the LORD your God commanded you to walk. So you shall purge the evil from among you" (Deuteronomy 13:4–5).

God exposes the heart of rebellion. We are to avoid and expose any prophet or dreamer of dreams who leads in a way that is contrary to God's word.

3 Dreams – Judges to Prophets

After 430 years in Egypt, the people of Israel left and eventually established themselves in the Promised Land, Canaan. God continued to speak through dreams to the judges and kings who ruled Israel, as well as the prophets.

Gideon's Encouragement

In the time of the judges the Midianites occupied Israel. God told Gideon that he was sending him to rescue Israel. Knowing that Gideon was plagued by doubts and fears, God told him to sneak into the Midian camp and listen to what the Midianite soldiers were saying about him.

> "When Gideon came, behold, a man was relating a dream to his friend. And he said, 'Behold, I had a dream; a loaf of barley bread was tumbling into the camp of Midian, and it came to the tent and struck it so that it fell, and turned it upside down so that the tent lay flat.' His friend replied, 'This is nothing less than the sword of Gideon the son of Joash, a man of Israel; God has given Midian and all the camp into his hand'" (Judges 7:13–14).

You can imagine how this dream and interpretation encouraged Gideon. Even his enemies acknowledged that God would help him win the battle. Gideon gave thanks to God and upon his return to camp, told the Israelite soldiers: "Arise, for the LORD has given the camp of Midian into your hands" (Judges 7:15).

So here we have an example of how God not only spoke to his people, but also to their enemies, all in an effort to counsel and encourage one of his leaders. And Gideon, with only three hundred men, defeated an enemy that vastly outnumbered them.

Saul's Distress

A few hundred years later, Israel had its first king, Saul, who gradually began to disobey God. Frustrated, as he sensed the anointing of God leaving him, Saul sought out a medium, imploring her to summon forth the spirit of the dead prophet Samuel. A figure of Samuel appeared and Saul appealed to him for advice.

> "I am greatly distressed; for the Philistines are waging war against me, and God has departed from me and no longer answers me, either through prophets or by dreams; therefore I have called you, that you may make known to me what I should do" (1 Samuel 28:15).

This illustrates how common it was in those days for God to speak to his people through dreams, especially the leaders. God regularly gave counsel on all sorts of matters through dreams, even military strategy. When that ceased because of his sins, Saul panicked and sinned yet again by seeking counsel from the dead, a practice strictly forbidden by the Mosaic Law.[18] God exposed Saul's sins and rebelliousness by no longer speaking to him through dreams and prophets.

> "Samuel said, 'Why then do you ask me, since the LORD has departed from you and has become your adversary? The LORD has done accordingly as He spoke through me; for the LORD has torn the kingdom out of your hand and given it to your neighbor, to David. As you did not obey the LORD and did not execute His fierce wrath on Amalek, so the LORD has done this thing to you this day'" (1 Samuel 28:16–18).

While alive, Samuel had warned Saul that because of his continued disobedience, God would take the kingdom from him and give it to David. We can only speculate what would have happened had Saul repented of his rebelliousness. However, he didn't, and Samuel's godly counsel was fulfilled.

Solomon's Promise

> "In Gibeon the LORD appeared to Solomon in a dream at night; and God said, 'Ask what you wish me to give you'" (1 Kings 3:5).

David succeeded Saul as king and then David's son, Solomon, took the throne. In this verse we see God using a dream and a leading question to expose Solomon's godly character. Sometimes I (Dianne), ponder what my response would be if the Lord appeared to me in a dream and asked, "Dianne, what do you wish me to give you?" My first thoughts might go to many selfish things. Solomon, however, replied by acknowledging the things God had already done.

> "Then Solomon said, 'You have shown great lovingkindness to Your servant David my father, according as he walked before You in truth and righteousness and uprightness of heart toward You; and You have reserved for him this great lovingkindness, that You have given him a son to sit on his throne, as it is this day'" (1 Kings

3:6).

Then Solomon humbly asked for his heart's desire.

> "Now, O LORD my God, You have made Your servant king in place of my father David, yet I am but a little child; I do not know how to go out or come in. Your servant is in the midst of Your people which You have chosen, a great people who are too many to be numbered or counted. So give Your servant an understanding heart to judge Your people to discern between good and evil. For who is able to judge this great people of Yours?" (1 Kings 3:7–9).

Imagine! The question from God in this dream gave opportunity to reveal Solomon's heart. His response was to ask for things that concern the heart-understanding in order that he might judge the people he ruled and discernment to know right from wrong. God was pleased with such a request.

> "It was pleasing in the sight of the Lord that Solomon had asked this thing. God said to him, 'Because you have asked this thing and have not asked for yourself long life, nor have asked riches for yourself, nor have you asked for the life of your enemies, but have asked for yourself discernment to understand justice, behold, I have done according to your words. Behold, I have given you a wise and discerning heart, so that there has been no one like you before you, nor shall one like you arise after you.
>
> "'I have also given you what you have not asked, both riches and honor, so that there will not be any among the kings like you all your days. If you walk in My ways, keeping My statutes and commandments, as your father David walked, then I will prolong your days'" (1 Kings 3:10–14).

God used this dream as a test, and because Solomon's

requests pleased God, he gave him far more than he asked for—blessings, wisdom, and material riches beyond his imagination. All this occurred through a dream.

Elihu's Counsel

> "Indeed God speaks once, Or twice, yet no one notices it. In a dream, a vision of the night, When sound sleep falls on men, While they slumber in their beds, Then He opens the ears of men, And seals their instruction, That He may turn man aside from his conduct, And keep man from pride; He keeps back his soul from the pit, And his life from passing over into Sheol" (Job 33:14–18).

These verses give some important insights into God's use of dreams and visions for counsel and healing. There is often a progression of sorts in God's approach to us. As these verses illustrate, God loves his children so much that he will get their attention one way or another, speaking once or twice. Sadly, we also see that often no one listens to him. So then, it is when "sound sleep falls," that God "opens the ears" for the purpose of sealing their instruction, counsel, or advice.

It is marvelous to think that in the night when we "slumber in our beds," our God speaks to us. This method of communicating bypasses the human need to analyze, figure things out, or control events. God connects with us, Spirit-to-spirit, to "turn man aside from his conduct, and keep man from pride." He also desires to "keep back his soul from the pit, and his life from passing over into Sheol." We need God to purge pride from our hearts, as otherwise it can take our soul to the pit and lead us into miserable places. God uses dreams to reveal these problems so that we will yield to him for healing.

Counsel to False Prophets

God strongly condemns those who prophesy falsely in his name using dreams. He does not send them, nor do they benefit his people.

> "I have heard what the prophets have said who prophesy falsely in My name, saying, 'I had a dream, I had a dream!' How long? Is there anything in the hearts of the prophets who prophesy falsehood, even these prophets of the deception of their own heart, who intend to make My people forget My name by their dreams which they relate to one another, just as their fathers forgot My name because of Baal? The prophet who has a dream may relate his dream, but let him who has My word speak My word in truth. What does straw have in common with grain? declares the LORD. 'Is not My word like fire?' declares the LORD, 'and like a hammer which shatters a rock?
>
> "'Therefore behold, I am against the prophets,' declares the LORD, 'who steal My words from each other. Behold, I am against the prophets,' declares the LORD, 'who use their tongues and declare, "The Lord declares." Behold, I am against those who have prophesied false dreams,' declares the LORD, 'and related them and led My people astray by their falsehoods and reckless boasting; yet I did not send them or command them, nor do they furnish this people the slightest benefit,' declares the LORD" (Jeremiah 23:25–32).

Their motive, God says, is to use dreams to lead his people astray and to forget his name. This excerpt seems to indicate that false prophets are free to relate their dreams, but God reminds us that his word is the standard by which we evaluate the interpretation of any dream. We must apply God's word. A dream may be authentic, but still have a false interpretation.

Dreams — Judges to Prophets

> "For thus says the LORD of hosts, the God of Israel, 'Do not let your prophets who are in your midst and your diviners deceive you, and do not listen to the dreams which they dream. For they prophesy falsely to you in My name; I have not sent them,' declares the LORD. For thus says the LORD, 'When seventy years have been completed for Babylon, I will visit you and fulfill My good word to you, to bring you back to this place. For I know the plans that I have for you,' declares the LORD, 'plans for welfare and not for calamity to give you a future and a hope.'" (Jeremiah 29:8–11).

God once again counsels strongly against those who use dreams for their own purposes, leading God's people away from him. Their hearts are full of deception and their understanding and application of the dreams are for their own means. The sad reality is that they speak in the name of the Lord but he has not sent them. Yet in the midst of this warning, God graciously counsels the faithful of his people that he has plans for them that will benefit their future and hope.

The Heart of the King

> "But as for me, this secret has not been revealed to me because I have more wisdom than anyone living, but for our sakes who make known the interpretation to the king, and that you may know the thoughts of your heart" (Daniel 2:30 NKJV™).

The Israelites strayed from God and were eventually defeated in battle by the Babylonians, who occupied their land and took many of them to Babylon in chains. Among the Israelite captives was a gifted young man, Daniel, who received special training in the court of the Babylonian ruler, King Nebuchadnezzar. One day the king had a dream that only Daniel was able to recall and interpret.

> "You, O king, were looking and behold, there was a single great statue; that statue, which was large and of extraordinary splendor, was standing in front of you, and its appearance was awesome. The head of that statue was made of fine gold, its breast and its arms of silver, its belly and its thighs of bronze, its legs of iron, its feet partly of iron and partly of clay.
>
> "You continued looking until a stone was cut out without hands, and it struck the statue on its feet of iron and clay and crushed them. Then the iron, the clay, the bronze, the silver and the gold were crushed all at the same time and became like chaff from the summer threshing floors; and the wind carried them away so that not a trace of them was found. But the stone that struck the statue became a great mountain and filled the whole earth" (Daniel 2:31–35).

After describing the dream, Daniel was able to give the king the interpretation. The head of gold represented the greatness of his present kingdom. The next kingdom, represented by silver, would be inferior. The third kingdom, represented by bronze, would be still weaker and yet still rule over the earth. The fourth kingdom, represented by iron, breaks in pieces. Finally, when all of the kingdoms have been destroyed, God will establish a kingdom that no one can destroy. Daniel ends with these words:

> "Inasmuch as you saw that a stone was cut out of the mountain without hands and that it crushed the iron, the bronze, the clay, the silver and the gold, the great God has made known to the king what will take place in the future; so the dream is true and its interpretation is trustworthy" (Daniel 2:45).

God used this dream to inform his people about events many years in the future—things we see unfolding today. In the end times, a kingdom above all kingdoms will emerge from a king's lineage. It will be the last kingdom—one that cannot be destroyed. This has encouraged many of God's people over the centuries. The king reacts to this interpretation by promoting and rewarding Daniel and acknowledging his God as the God of gods.

Driven to Repentance

King Nebuchadnezzar had another vision that caused him to fear, as he could not interpret it. After consulting his court magicians and astrologers in vain, he called for Daniel and recounted the dream to him.

> "Now these were the visions in my mind as I lay on my bed: I was looking, and behold, there was a tree in the midst of the earth and its height was great. The tree grew large and became strong And its height reached to the sky, And it was visible to the end of the whole earth. Its foliage was beautiful and its fruit abundant, And in it was food for all. The beasts of the field found shade under it, And the birds of the sky dwelt in its branches, And all living creatures fed themselves from it.
>
> "I was looking in the visions in my mind as I lay on my bed, and behold, an angelic watcher, a holy one, descended from heaven. He shouted out and spoke as follows: 'Chop down the tree and cut off its branches, Strip off its foliage and scatter its fruit; Let the beasts flee from under it And the birds from its branches.
>
> "'Yet leave the stump with its roots in the ground, But with a band of iron and bronze around it In the new grass of the field; And let him be drenched with the dew of heaven, And let him share with the beasts in the grass of the earth. Let his mind be changed from that of a man And let a beast's mind be given to him, And let seven periods of time pass over him.
>
> "'This sentence is by the decree of the angelic watchers

And the decision is a command of the holy ones, In order that the living may know That the Most High is ruler over the realm of mankind, And bestows it on whom He wishes And sets over it the lowliest of men'" (Daniel 4:10–17).

The pressure was on! The interpretation troubled Daniel and he hesitated to relate it, knowing that it was not favorable toward the king. However, Nebuchadnezzar encouraged him, and so he proceeded.

"The tree that you saw, which became large and grew strong, whose height reached to the sky and was visible to all the earth and whose foliage was beautiful and its fruit abundant, and in which was food for all, under which the beasts of the field dwelt and in whose branches the birds of the sky lodged–it is you, O king; for you have become great and grown strong, and your majesty has become great and reached to the sky and your dominion to the end of the earth.

"In that the king saw an angelic watcher, a holy one, descending from heaven and saying, 'Chop down the tree and destroy it; yet leave the stump with its roots in the ground, but with a band of iron and bronze around it in the new grass of the field, and let him be drenched with the dew of heaven, and let him share with the beasts of the field until seven periods of time pass over him,'

"this is the interpretation, O king, and this is the decree of the Most High, which has come upon my lord the king: that you be driven away from mankind and your dwelling place be with the beasts of the field, and you be given grass to eat like cattle and be drenched with the dew of heaven; and seven periods of time will pass over you, until you recognize that the Most High is ruler over the realm of mankind and bestows it on whomever He wishes.

"And in that it was commanded to leave the stump with the roots of the tree, your kingdom will be assured to you after you recognize that it is Heaven that rules" (Daniel 4:20–26).

This dream contains strong elements of counsel and healing. It clearly demonstrated that the king was too proud, considering himself the supreme ruler of the land while failing to acknowledge God. Therefore, God stated that these events would take place "in order that the living may know that the Most High is ruler over the realm of mankind, And bestows it on whom He wishes And sets over it the lowliest of men" (Daniel 4:17).

Daniel in his wisdom then advised the king to repent from his sins and to do righteousness and mercy to the poor. God may possibly spare him. God had even provided the way out of this tragedy if only the king would listen and act accordingly.

"Therefore, O king, may my advice be pleasing to you: break away now from your sins by doing righteousness and from your iniquities by showing mercy to the poor, in case there may be a prolonging of your prosperity" (Daniel 4:27).

Sadly, the king chose not to heed the counsel of the Lord or that of his servant Daniel. He continued to rule with pride and arrogance, the very sins of which God was trying to heal him. He soon suffered the consequences.

"All this happened to Nebuchadnezzar the king. Twelve months later he was walking on the roof of the royal palace of Babylon. The king reflected and said, 'Is this not Babylon the great, which I myself have built as a royal residence by the might of my power and for the glory of my majesty?'

"While the word was in the king's mouth, a voice came

from heaven, saying, 'King Nebuchadnezzar, to you it is declared: sovereignty has been removed from you, and you will be driven away from mankind, and your dwelling place will be with the beasts of the field. You will be given grass to eat like cattle, and seven periods of time will pass over you until you recognize that the Most High is ruler over the realm of mankind and bestows it on whomever He wishes.'

"Immediately the word concerning Nebuchadnezzar was fulfilled; and he was driven away from mankind and began eating grass like cattle, and his body was drenched with the dew of heaven until his hair had grown like eagles' feathers and his nails like birds' claws" (Daniel 4:28–33).

Eventually, just as the Lord had revealed in the dream, Nebuchadnezzar was restored.

"But at the end of that period, I, Nebuchadnezzar, raised my eyes toward heaven and my reason returned to me, and I blessed the Most High and praised and honored Him who lives forever; For His dominion is an everlasting dominion, And His kingdom endures from generation to generation. All the inhabitants of the earth are accounted as nothing, But He does according to His will in the host of heaven And among the inhabitants of earth; And no one can ward off His hand Or say to Him, 'What have You done?'" (Daniel 4:34–35).

The results of blessing and restoration were immediate:

"At that time my reason returned to me. And my majesty and splendor were restored to me for the glory of my kingdom, and my counselors and my nobles began seeking me out; so I was reestablished in my sovereignty, and surpassing greatness was added to me. Now I, Nebuchadnezzar, praise, exalt and honor the

King of heaven, for all His works are true and His ways just, and He is able to humble those who walk in pride" (Daniel 4:36–37).

What can we learn from this story? We have a God who loves us too much to let us continue blindly in our sinful ways, so he sometimes chastises us in order to bring healing into our lives. He disciplines those he loves.[19]

Future Events

We should be thankful that Daniel was obedient and wrote down his dreams. This is the dream of four creatures:

> "In the first year of Belshazzar king of Babylon Daniel saw a dream and visions in his mind as he lay on his bed; then he wrote the dream down and related the following summary of it. Daniel said, 'I was looking in my vision by night, and behold, the four winds of heaven were stirring up the great sea. And four great beasts were coming up from the sea, different from one another. The first was like a lion and had the wings of an eagle. I kept looking until its wings were plucked, and it was lifted up from the ground and made to stand on two feet like a man; a human mind also was given to it.
>
> "'And behold, another beast, a second one, resembling a bear. And it was raised up on one side, and three ribs were in its mouth between its teeth; and thus they said to it, "Arise, devour much meat!" After this I kept looking, and behold, another one, like a leopard, which had on its back four wings of a bird; the beast also had four heads, and dominion was given to it.
>
> "'After this I kept looking in the night visions, and behold, a fourth beast, dreadful and terrifying and extremely strong; and it had large iron teeth. It devoured and crushed and trampled down the remainder with its feet; and it was different from all the beasts that were

before it, and it had ten horns. While I was contemplating the horns, behold, another horn, a little one, came up among them, and three of the first horns were pulled out by the roots before it; and behold, this horn possessed eyes like the eyes of a man and a mouth uttering great boasts'" (Daniel 7:1–8).

Enter the Ancient of Days:

"I kept looking Until thrones were set up, And the Ancient of Days took His seat; His vesture was like white snow And the hair of His head like pure wool. His throne was ablaze with flames, Its wheels were a burning fire. A river of fire was flowing And coming out from before Him; Thousands upon thousands were attending Him, And myriads upon myriads were standing before Him; The court sat, And the books were opened.

"Then I kept looking because of the sound of the boastful words which the horn was speaking; I kept looking until the beast was slain, and its body was destroyed and given to the burning fire. As for the rest of the beasts, their dominion was taken away, but an extension of life was granted to them for an appointed period of time.

"I kept looking in the night visions, And behold, with the clouds of heaven One like a Son of Man was coming, And He came up to the Ancient of Days And was presented before Him. And to Him was given dominion, Glory and a kingdom, That all the peoples, nations and men of every language Might serve Him. His dominion is an everlasting dominion Which will not pass away; And His kingdom is one Which will not be destroyed" (Daniel 7:9–14).

Daniel's spirit is not at peace until he receives the interpretation.

"As for me, Daniel, my spirit was distressed within me,

and the visions in my mind kept alarming me. I approached one of those who were standing by and began asking him the exact meaning of all this. So he told me and made known to me the interpretation of these things: 'These great beasts, which are four in number, are four kings who will arise from the earth. But the saints of the Highest One will receive the kingdom and possess the kingdom forever, for all ages to come.'

"Then I desired to know the exact meaning of the fourth beast, which was different from all the others, exceedingly dreadful, with its teeth of iron and its claws of bronze, and which devoured, crushed and trampled down the remainder with its feet, and the meaning of the ten horns that were on its head and the other horn which came up, and before which three of them fell, namely, that horn which had eyes and a mouth uttering great boasts and which was larger in appearance than its associates.

"I kept looking, and that horn was waging war with the saints and overpowering them until the Ancient of Days came and judgment was passed in favor of the saints of the Highest One, and the time arrived when the saints took possession of the kingdom.

"Thus he said: 'The fourth beast will be a fourth kingdom on the earth, which will be different from all the other kingdoms and will devour the whole earth and tread it down and crush it. As for the ten horns, out of this kingdom ten kings will arise; and another will arise after them, and he will be different from the previous ones and will subdue three kings.

"'He will speak out against the Most High and wear down the saints of the Highest One, and he will intend to make alterations in times and in law; and they will be given into his hand for a time, times, and half a time.

"'But the court will sit for judgment, and his dominion

will be taken away, annihilated and destroyed forever. Then the sovereignty, the dominion and the greatness of all the kingdoms under the whole heaven will be given to the people of the saints of the Highest One; His kingdom will be an everlasting kingdom, and all the dominions will serve and obey Him.' At this point the revelation ended. As for me, Daniel, my thoughts were greatly alarming me and my face grew pale, but I kept the matter to myself" (Daniel 7:15–28).

This dream and vision of the night is long and involved. Daniel had no role in the dream except to observe, which means the dream was for and about others. Daniel was being shown what was going to happen in the distant future, making it clear that God was in control of these events. At the end of the revelation, Daniel was greatly alarmed.

The Outpouring

"It will come about after this That I will pour out My Spirit on all mankind; And your sons and daughters will prophesy, Your old men will dream dreams, Your young men will see visions" (Joel 2:28).

Telling False Dreams

"For the teraphim speak iniquity, And the diviners see lying visions And tell false dreams; They comfort in vain. Therefore the people wander like sheep, They are afflicted, because there is no shepherd" (Zechariah 10:2).

The teraphim, or household idols, and diviners are lumped together as deceivers. When lying visions and false dreams abound, God's people pay a high price. They will become unfocused, wandering, and afflicted, when there are no godly leaders.

4   Dreams – New Testament

In the New Testament we find many examples of God speaking to his people through dreams, sometimes delivering important messages. Reading some of these accounts helps us better appreciate the place dreams and their messages have in God's plans.

Birth of Jesus

From our side of the cross we see Jesus as the ascended, glorified Son of God, seated at the right hand of God Almighty. No safer place exists. However, for a time Jesus was born as a helpless tiny baby as you and I. During that time he too needed protection, and from much more than most of us have needed.

> "But when he had considered this, behold, an angel of the Lord appeared to him in a dream, saying, 'Joseph, son of David, do not be afraid to take Mary as your wife; for the Child who has been conceived in her is of

the Holy Spirit. She will bear a Son; and you shall call His name Jesus, for He will save His people from their sins'" (Matthew 1:20-21).

Were it not for this dream, Jesus would have been born out of wedlock, assuming, of course, that Mary escaped stoning for her obvious inappropriate behavior.

> "And having been warned by God in a dream not to return to Herod, the magi left for their own country by another way" (Matthew 2:12).

The counsel that God gave to the Magi in the dream was vital to the existence of his son. If they had revealed Jesus' location to Herod, he may have had Jesus killed before Joseph and Mary could take him to Egypt. The esteem of the Magi for dreams caused them to obey and Herod did not get his way.

> "Now when they had gone, behold, an angel of the Lord appeared to Joseph in a dream and said, 'Get up! Take the Child and His mother and flee to Egypt, and remain there until I tell you; for Herod is going to search for the Child to destroy Him.' So Joseph got up and took the Child and His mother while it was still night, and left for Egypt" (Matthew 2:13–14).

Danger again lurked for Jesus. God used another dream to warn Joseph to take Jesus and Mary to another country for safety. Joseph obeyed.

> "But when Herod died, behold, an angel of the Lord appeared in a dream to Joseph in Egypt, and said, 'Get up, take the Child and His mother, and go into the land of Israel; for those who sought the Child's life are dead.' So Joseph got up, took the Child and His mother, and came into the land of Israel" (Matthew 2:19–21).

A few years later, through yet another dream, God counseled Joseph to return to Israel. Those who threatened

Jesus were dead. Joseph obeyed the dream and returned to Israel.

> "But when he [Joseph] heard that Archelaus was reigning over Judea in place of his father Herod, he was afraid to go there. Then after being warned by God in a dream, he left for the regions of Galilee, and came and lived in a city called Nazareth. This was to fulfill what was spoken through the prophets: 'He shall be called a Nazarene'" (Matthew 2:22–23).

This dream addressed an issue of fear. Because Joseph was afraid of going to Judea, God gave him a dream that brought both healing and counsel. Once again, Joseph obeyed God's counsel in the dream and went to Nazareth, where he settled with his family. In the process, his actions fulfilled what the prophets wrote about Jesus being a Nazarene.[20]

Church Growth

Imagine praying for direction and then an angel appears to you in a vision, telling you where to go and who to seek out for answers. This is what happened to Cornelius, a gentile believer in the book of Acts.

> "About the ninth hour of the day he clearly saw in a vision an angel of God who had just come in and said to him, 'Cornelius!' And fixing his gaze on him and being much alarmed, he said, 'What is it, Lord?' And he said to him, 'your prayers and alms have ascended as a memorial before God. Now dispatch some men to Joppa and send for a man named Simon, who is also called Peter; he is staying with a tanner named Simon, whose house is by the sea'" (Acts 10:3–6).

In this vision, the angel told Cornelius the location and name of the person he needed to contact. While the delegation of Cornelius' men was traveling to find Peter, God was preparing Peter for these unusual guests.

> "On the next day, as they were on their way and approaching the city, Peter went up on the housetop about the sixth hour to pray. But he became hungry and was desiring to eat; but while they were making preparations, he fell into a trance; and he saw the sky opened up, and an object like a great sheet coming down, lowered by four corners to the ground, and there were in it all kinds of four-footed animals and crawling creatures of the earth and birds of the air.
>
> "A voice came to him, 'Get up, Peter, kill and eat!' But Peter said, 'By no means, Lord, for I have never eaten anything unholy and unclean.' Again a voice came to him a second time, 'What God has cleansed, no longer consider unholy.' This happened three times, and immediately the object was taken up into the sky" (Acts 10:9–16).

Until this point, the early church consisted of Jewish Christians only. Most believers still held to the Jewish mindset that gentiles were "unclean" and excluded from salvation. In this dream, God was telling Peter that salvation was for gentiles as well. No one was to be excluded. Peter later expressed this to Cornelius, "I most certainly understand now that God is not one to show partiality, but in every nation the man who fears Him and does what is right is welcome to Him" (Acts 10:34–35).

This dream was a milestone in the life of the early church. God gave Peter counsel and because he accepted it and obeyed, spiritual healing in the form of the Gospel was ultimately brought to untold millions throughout the centuries.

Dreams — New Testament

Missions Venture

"A vision appeared to Paul in the night: a man of Macedonia was standing and appealing to him, and saying, 'Come over to Macedonia and help us.' When he had seen the vision, immediately we sought to go into Macedonia, concluding that God had called us to preach the gospel to them" (Acts 16:9–10).

In the book of Acts, we read of the Apostle Paul's many missionary trips. At one point, he needed direction and God spoke to him, telling him to change his plans and go to Macedonia. By obeying, Paul took the gospel message to some important cities, including Philippi and Thessalonica, which were gateways to Europe.

Revelation

The last book of the Bible, the book of Revelation, is an extended and detailed vision that Jesus gave to John the Apostle. Generally seen as a description of the end times, Revelations reassures believers that even in times of persecution and spiritual darkness, He is in control of events and we need not fear.

Conclusion

When listed, many people are amazed at the number of scriptures that pertain to dreams and visions in the Bible. During a seminar for pastors, some commented that they had read many of these passages before, but until then they had missed the connection to dreams and visions.

Through this study we trust it is clear that dreams have played an important role in God's plan and purposes. Does God esteem dreams? Did dreams play an important role in the development and execution of God's plans and purposes? Are dreams a versatile means of communication? The answer to these questions has to be 'yes.' From the first accounts of the oldest writings whether Abram or Job, to the Revelation of Jesus Christ to the Apostle John, dreams and visions played a significant role.

Has the role of dreams and visions in the lives of God's people ended? Has it been replaced, perhaps with the canon of scriptures that we have and those of old did not? Is all of God's counsel or all we need contained in the Bible?

Who is telling us that dreams and visions are no longer a means by which God communicates with us today? Certainly it is not the Bible that leads us to that conclusion, rather the opposite.

In the chapters that follow we will show many examples of the ways God uses dreams to counsel and heal his people today.

5   A Primer on Dream Types

There is a God in heaven who reveals mysteries (Daniel 2:28).

"It makes no sense."
"It's all over the place."
"I had a weird dream."
"This dream was really strange."
"It must have been something I ate."

Have you heard comments like this, or perhaps made them yourself regarding the symbols in dreams? As counselors and teachers on the subject, we hear them all the time. However, the comments often change when we help our clients—the dreamers—unravel the meaning of these seemingly mysterious symbols and develop the message.

"Wow, that's great!"
"That's a wonderful interpretation!"
"It makes a lot of sense when I have the interpretation."
"That speaks to where I am right now."
"What a tremendous encouragement!"

Have you ever watched a foreign language movie? Or listened to people having a conversation in a foreign language and wished you could understand them? Dreams are like that. They have their own language, and it is similar for all human beings—except that each of us has a unique "dialect" of sorts. That dialect consists of symbols that are personal to each dreamer—a personal dialect. In trying to understand symbols in dreams, it is important to view them from the standpoint of the dreamer, not anyone else. It makes all the difference between understanding the message of the dream and being misled.

When God wishes to speak to us in dreams, he uses the events and life experiences of the dreamer to create a short video representation of a message he wants her to receive. He uses our personal experiences because he wants us to understand the personal message. The symbols he uses in our dreams are personal, for our personal understanding. That seems simple enough, so why do we often have so much difficulty understanding them?

In a dream, we have a Spirit-to-spirit connection—God's Spirit to our spirit. Our often-analytical minds are relatively inactive as we sleep so the message can be transmitted clearly, with little interference from our minds.

We believe that the process of learning to understand our dreams begins with a respect for them. If we can't be bothered with dreams, God will not bother us with them; but if we are interested, we may find that they can lead us into a deeper relationship with him. As we learn to understand and respond to the messages of our dreams, we inevitably grow spiritually and into the image of Jesus—the predestined goal of the Father for us.

A Primer on Dream Types

Dream Categories

In our work, we generally use two categories of dreams: message dreams and miscellaneous dreams. Message dreams are characterized as being succinct and complete, including symbols that are significant to the dreamer. Miscellaneous dreams by contrast, have stories and symbols that seem to be random, with no pattern to them. They often appear to be something of a mental "defrag" of a busy day or things the body is going through. "Defrag" is an abbreviated computer process of taking fragments of data that may have been stored in a scattered way on the hard drive and defragmenting them, by drawing them together in their logical order. In other words, it is a mental house cleaning of the events of a busy day.

Our focus is on understanding message dreams.

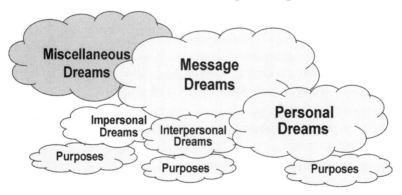

Types of Message Dreams

Our experience and extensive biblical examination has led us to conclude that there are different types of message dreams. If we are to have any success with our interpretations, we must first identify which type the dream falls into. So far, we have identified three main types of dreams and a fourth that pertains to children:

45

1. Personal. Dreams that have a message for the dreamer.
2. Impersonal. Dreams that have a message for someone other than the dreamer.
3. Interpersonal. Dreams that have a message for someone other than the dreamer, but which also affect the dreamer.
4. Dreams for caregivers. We discuss these in Chapter 12.

In *Dream Dreams*, we referred to the first three types as subjective, objective, and combination dreams. In this book we have renamed these; referring to them as personal (subjective), impersonal (objective), or interpersonal (combination) dreams. This seems to us to be simpler and more clearly identifies the core characteristic of each type. We have found these types in the dreams of the Bible.

To determine if a dream is personal, impersonal, or interpersonal, determine what your role was in the dream. Were you active, observing only, or active for a portion of the dream with a clear transition to simply being an observer? If you were:

- active throughout, it is a personal dream—for and about you, regardless of those you may know in the dream
- strictly observing, it is an impersonal dream—for and about others
- active and then observing (or visa versa), it is an interpersonal dream—primarily for and about others, but affecting you

Does this approach overly-categorize God, putting him in a box? We don't think so. We read in the Bible of a God who is not the author of disorder or confusion.[21] His workings, both in the physical and spiritual realms, are characterized by identifiable patterns and principles. Given the numerous occasions in which God has communicated important messages through dreams and visions, we don't find it unreasonable to expect that he has imposed a certain order on them. To deny any order, any rhyme or reason, is to open the door to chaos, allowing us to make our dreams say whatever suits us. With this in mind, we consider the general categories of personal, impersonal, and interpersonal dreams as valid types that are based on scriptural examples.

Conclusion

Understanding the difference between miscellaneous and message dreams helps us decide which dreams to record and try to interpret. Our understanding of the different types of message dreams—personal, impersonal, and interpersonal—further simplifies the interpretation process.

Symbols fill our dreams. God uses them as a unique picture language to communicate a message to us. In the next chapter we will learn more about understanding the symbols—the snakes, trucks, planes and many other objects—that show up in our dreams. These examples will help us develop insights into various symbols and better equip us to decode God's messages for us.

Steve & Dianne Bydeley

6   Symbols in Dreams – A Primer

Symbols mean different things to different people. A homeowner may view her house as her castle, her safe haven from the worries and cares of the world. She will probably also treat it as her largest earthly investment. To the contractor who built it, however, it is just one of hundreds of nearly indistinguishable projects. Similarly, a pilot views an airplane quite differently from someone who has never flown. So it is with the symbols in our dreams: each one has a unique significance to the dreamer.

Personal Dreams

Approximately 90–95 percent of our dreams are of a personal nature—for and about the dreamer. It follows then that the symbols in these dreams and their meanings are personal to the dreamer. What we mean by this is that God has used the life and experiences of the dreamer in selecting the symbols for the dream. They have personal relevance to the dreamer, who alone holds the key to understanding their meaning. The correct interpretation of these symbols can only belong to the dreamer, not to those helping to interpret. Even if someone helping a dreamer has a gift for interpreting dreams, their interpretation should still receive confirmation, an inner knowing, from within the spirit of the dreamer.

For example, I once had a dream of a koala. Most people in North America probably do not dream of koalas because they have never encountered one. In my case, the koala became a personal symbol because of an upcoming trip to Australia—the only place in the world where koalas live. Some people like dogs while others fear them. Those different feelings about dogs significantly influence the meaning of any symbol related to dogs.

When trying to understand dreams, always look for a personal connection to the symbol. Whenever we dream of cars, one of the first questions we ask is: "What side was the steering wheel on?" Because we lived in Australia for a year, this has become an important personal detail in our dreams.

Impersonal or Interpersonal Dreams

An impersonal dream is for and about others and an interpersonal dream is for and about others, but its message affects the dreamer by association. In these dreams, the meanings of the symbols belong to those to whom God has given the dream—not the dreamer. Generally, less then one out of ten dreams may be impersonal or interpersonal. Because of this, we will offer only a brief explanation about them, devoting most of our time to personal dreams.

Impersonal Dreams

Impersonal dreams are easy to identify because the dreamer is not active in the dream, apart from watching. In the seventh chapter of Daniel, verses two and three, we find an example of an impersonal dream.

> "Daniel said, 'I was looking in my vision by night, and behold, the four winds of heaven were stirring up the great sea. And four great beasts were coming up from the sea, different from one another.'"

As the vision unfolds, Daniel repeatedly uses the phrase; "I kept looking..." indicating that he did not enter into the activity of the vision. At the end, Daniel approaches an angel who gives him the interpretation. This dream was not about Daniel, but about the future beyond his lifetime. It was intended for others, not Daniel.

Interpersonal Dreams

Interpersonal dreams are a bit harder to identify. An example would be Joseph's dream of the sheaves.

> "We were binding sheaves in the field, and lo, my sheaf rose up and also stood erect; and behold, your sheaves gathered around and bowed down to my sheaf" (Genesis 37:7).

Joseph started with the words "We were binding sheaves in the field." This indicates an active role at the beginning of the dream. Then, as an observer, he goes on to describe the activities of the sheaves. His brothers' sheaves encircle and bow to his sheave, which remains erect, doing nothing. When Joseph tells his brothers of this dream, they understand that the sheaves represent them, exclaiming, "Are you actually going to reign over us? Or are you really going to rule over us" (Genesis 37:8)? The dream is for and about Joseph's brothers, but it does affect him.

Responding to Impersonal and Interpersonal Dreams

When we have an impersonal or interpersonal dream, we should pray for guidance in determining whom the dream is for and if God gave us the dream for intercession or intervention. By intercession we mean that God wants us to pray for those that the dream is about, and by intervention, are we to approach and give the dream to those for whom God has given us the dream.

It is always safe to pray or intercede for those that the dream is about. In this case, God has brought to us an issue in someone's life or an organization for which he wants us to pray, and only pray, until we no longer feel a burden or concern for them. If, after prayer, we believe God wants us to intervene, then pray for God's timing, guidance, and humility in approaching those for whom God has given the dream. When we approach them, simply give them the dream.

If they are in a church body, consider meeting first with their pastor/leader, requesting permission to give the dream to that person.[22] If the pastor/leader does not give you permission, then your responsibility in this situation is over, except to continue to pray for the individual. If you receive permission to approach the person, then give them a written account of the dream. Remember, the symbols are personal and relevant to them; it is their dream to understand, not yours.

Your task is complete, so do nothing more unless asked. This includes respecting the person's privacy and not mentioning the dream to others. If God had wanted the dream to be public knowledge, he could have used a newspaper. In everything you do, in every decision you make, be sure to honor the individual and avoid imposing anything on the dreamer.

Dream Symbols in Personal Dreams

The symbols in impersonal and interpersonal dreams contain meanings that belong to those who the dream is

Symbols in Dreams—A Primer

for—not the dreamer. This precludes the need for the dreamer to attempt to interpret them. Personal dreams are different. In this section, we offer some guidelines to understanding general symbols in personal dreams.

We stress that these are guidelines. We cannot and should not pretend that we can offer nicely defined meanings for symbols. They are, after all, unique—personal to the life and experiences of the dreamer. In the chapters that follow, we will look at the interpretation of dream symbols that are specific to God's counsel and healing.

To understand the meaning of symbols in personal dreams (hereafter simply referred to as the dream), try following these steps:

- Make a list of all the images, emotions, feelings, and actions that were present in the dream.

- Give some thought to the context of the dream—the things that were happening in your life around the time of the dream. Context often holds the key to understanding the message. Look back several days if necessary. Old dreams are often difficult to interpret as we have forgotten important details of context. Of course, some dreams are not related to events in our lives, so be prepared to look beyond the context of your life when there is no apparent relevance.

- After you have looked at the context, look again at each symbol on your list, searching for relevance, for something that catches your attention. If there is a connection, things may begin to unfold. If there is no connection, you will need to dig deeper.

The images God used in your dream come from your life and experiences and therefore, the correct meaning of each symbol is within you. For example, we worked with a doctor who regularly had images related to hospitals in his dreams. Similarly, a teacher regularly dreamed of things related to the classroom. The meaning of those symbols naturally belonged to these individuals since we, as counselors, could not relate to those experiences. We could however, ask questions of the dreamer, hoping to draw from them the meaning of the symbols. There have been occasions where one of us has received a dream with symbols that were not personal, not relevant, until days or weeks later. At that time, the meaning of the dream unfolded.

Most of our dreams are symbolic and God weaves the message through those symbols. For example, you are probably familiar with Aesop's tale about the race between the hare and the tortoise. It provides an interesting story in itself, but even more interesting is the message that the author wove into the tale. The hare and the tortoise represent or symbolize two human character types. Unless we understand that, we do not fully benefit from the message. Once we do factor that in, the message is clearly absorbed—slow and steady wins the race.

In the same way, our dreams have messages woven into the images that symbolize or represent something crucial to understanding the message. Does logic work as a means of interpreting the symbols? Usually not. Is it logical that a hare or a tortoise would represent human character qualities, that three little pigs would represent qualities of hard-work and foresight in humans, or that sheep or a lost coin would represent people? If we are going to understand these symbols, we, as dreamers, need to take a more creative, abstract, or anointed approach to the symbols in our dreams. We need to reach into our life experiences for clues.

Left/Right Brain Activities

Extensive research has established that we use the left

Symbols in Dreams—A Primer

side of our brain for logic, sequences, history, and mathematics, while we use the right side for creativity, emotions, imagination, and artistic endeavors. Some people are predominantly left-brain thinkers, some right, and some seem to move easily between the two. Right-brain thinkers and those who can switch seem to have a better grasp of the symbolism of dreams and their interpretations. They seem better able to avoid the limitations of rigid, logical, thinking patterns. The following chart illustrates how differently left-brain and right-brain thinkers might interpret similar symbols.

Image	The Logic Left	The Creative Right
House	A building, structure, dwelling	Where I live, my life, me
Kitchen	Food preparation, appliances	Where I eat or am fed
Bathroom	Place to clean or relieve myself	Refreshment, inner and outer cleaning
Car	Transportation, mechanical	The active part of my life, me
Bear	Wild animal, omnivore, hibernates	Rage, danger, control, or cuddly

It seems that God interfaces more with the right side of the brain when communicating through dreams and visions. Dreams are inherently a creative, artistic endeavor produced by a creative and artistic God using the plot, set, and cast that he chooses from our life experiences. To truly understand these elements and connect symbols with meaning, we must use our right-brain creative abilities.

How do we cross over into the right, creative side of our brain? Some do it easily, while others have to work at it.

When you look at the clouds, do you see rain, condensation, and dew point; or do you see shapes and patterns? It is difficult for logical left-brain thinkers to make any kind of switch, because they immediately want a formula or a sequence of steps to follow, which in itself defeats the process.

When I (Steve) taught photography as a general interest course at college, I gave the students one exercise that helped them cross over. The instructions were that they take one roll of 36 exposure film and fill the roll with pictures of their bathroom. Invariably they reported taking the first half of the roll on the obvious (logical) stuff, and then they forced themselves to look for pictures, create images and abstract designs. They worked hard on the last pictures, but were rewarded by learning ways of seeing things they had not experienced before.

Work at encouraging your brain to cross over and exercise the right side for a while. Your family and friends will probably enjoy the changes.

Literal Dreams

Literal dreams contain no symbolism that requires interpretation. Although most dreams are not literal, the Bible gives us some examples. These include Abimelech's dream, where God called him a "dead man" for taking Abraham's wife,[23] and in the New Testament, the dreams God gave Joseph in order to protect the infant Jesus.[24] Perhaps the recorders of these events gave us the interpretation of the dream and not the actual dream. However, in both examples the message demanded immediate action. Were that necessary in our lives, we believe the message of the dream would be immediately clear as well.

Recording Your Dreams

Always write down your dreams as soon as possible after you receive them. We see this diligence in the prophet Daniel, who recorded the dreams and visions he received from God. Over the millenniums, untold millions have benefited from his obedience.

> "In the first year of Belshazzar king of Babylon Daniel saw a dream and visions in his mind as he lay on his bed; then he wrote the dream down and related the following summary of it" (Daniel 7:1).

Our personal experience has been that dreams often fade quickly from our memories. Because of this, we regularly pray that God will wake us after a dream so that we can record the details while they are fresh. Even when he does wake us, however, it requires will power to write the dream down. Too often we have slept through a dream and woke in the morning, knowing that we had an important dream but not being able to recall the details. A message from God to us deserves a better response than rolling over and going back to sleep. Be diligent in recording your dreams.

Conclusion

As a primer on dream interpretation, we have proposed three main dream types, personal—for and about the dreamer, impersonal—for and about others, and interpersonal—for and about others but affecting you.

In the personal dream, symbols come out of the life experiences of the dreamer and often relate to the events in their life at the time of the dream.

As we move on to the topic of healing dream symbols, it is important to be familiar with these general interpretation principles.

When a child is ill, nothing is more important to a parent than a speedy recovery. God, more than an earthly parent, is interested in our well-being. He wants us to be spiritually and emotionally healthy and to experience an abundant life that is full of joy and peace. Jesus paid a high price to provide these things for us, and God goes to great lengths to ensure we experience them. We have found that he often uses dreams to counsel us and bring about spiritual healing.

7   Counseled in the Night

> I will bless the LORD who has counseled me; Indeed, my mind instructs me in the night (Psalm 16:7).

Black Dog

A friend who is involved in Christian ministry shared this dream with me.

"My husband and I were in a car. While we were talking, from the corner of my eye, I noticed something dark enter through the left-hand-side back window. After my husband got out of the car, a small black dog jumped from the back seat into my lap and firmly bit my left hand. When I finally freed my hand, he latched onto my right hand. After what felt like forever, I managed to get free and run out of the car to find my husband."

When I began to ask this friend about the context of her life and especially her Christian ministry, it became evident to her that this was a warning about an intrusion that might disrupt the work of her hands. As we continued talking about the dream, she mentioned that a new member in the ministry in which she was involved had caused some disruption in a former church. We concluded that if she prayed against the intrusion of whomever this little dog represented, then the work of her hands would continue to prosper. Would information like that be a benefit to your ministry or your church?

Counsel

Counsel can be defined as advice or guidance given, usually by someone with greater understanding. God fills that condition and he does counsel and instruct us in the night.

> "A vision appeared to Paul in the night: a man of Macedonia was standing and appealing to him, and saying, 'Come over to Macedonia and help us.' When he had seen the vision, immediately we sought to go into Macedonia, concluding that God had called us to preach the gospel to them. So putting out to sea from Troas, we ran a straight course to Samothrace, and on the day following to Neapolis; and from there to Philippi, which is a leading city of the district of Macedonia, a Roman colony; and we were staying in this city for some days" (Acts 16:9–12).

These verses and this concept are important, especially for Christian leaders. When we review the dreams of the Bible, we see that God gave significant dreams of direction to those who were leaders of families,[25] nations,[26] churches,[27] and as in Paul's case above, mission organizations.

Supported Walk

"I was walking through a field and came upon a river. It was very wide and I wondered how I was going to cross over to the other side. I heard someone say, 'Just keep walking.' So I stepped out and found myself walking on top of the water. I wondered how this was possible and so I looked down. There, just under the surface of the water, I saw an angel. Everywhere I placed my foot the angel's hand was there, holding me up. I soon found I had crossed the river."

As the pastor from Kenya told me this dream, I could see the sparkle and joy in his eyes.

"What did the dream mean to you?" I asked.

"No matter what obstacles I faced at that time, I could count on my Jesus seeing me through to the other side," Robert replied decisively.

"Are dreams important to you?" I queried.

"I wouldn't want to be in the ministry without dreams to help me. Yes, they're important to me," Robert replied with conviction.

His response to my questions was in sharp contrast to many replies I received while attending a conference for pastors from Africa and North America. As I interviewed them, it became clear that those from Africa had a high regard for dreams, while those from North America generally did not. In many ways we North Americans need the counsel, guidance, and encouragement that can come from God through our dreams.

Leaving

A pastor recounted this dream:

"I was in a tall apartment building made of brick. I was standing in the opening of a large picture window where the glass had been removed. There were steps built into the wall of the building. As I was standing in the window, I saw a few people climb down the steps from the window to the ground. I didn't do anything but watch."

The tall apartment building represented the pastor's

congregation. Windows can often represent a prophetic gift, or in this case insight into some coming event. The steps outside the building and leading down to the ground were a way leading out.

This dream describes what happened a few days later. Two deacons in the church stepped down from their positions. Because of the dream, the pastor felt free to watch and not become discouraged. Because of the warning from the dream, it was not unexpected and he saw God working in the situation.

Relationships

"I saw Pat walking in a field and a large object blown by the wind hit her. Then I saw her behind a table under a tent. I went to see if she was all right. She was very mean and hateful to me."

This interpersonal dream (the dreamer was observing at first and then entered into the activity) helped a pastor understand the dynamics of a problem concerning his relationship with Pat, a woman who was active in the church. She was acting antagonistically towards him and he did not know why. In the dream she was behind the table—her work in the church. The incident in the field represented a difficulty Pat was having in her personal life, which was of the Holy Spirit (wind) as perhaps a form of discipline or a more direct attempt to get her attention.

Although God did not reveal Pat's problem to the pastor, he was able to pray for her in a general way and not interfere with the work God was doing in her life. The pastor also took consolation in knowing that, although Pat's hostility was directed at him, it was not for him. This made it much easier to extend grace to her.

Counseled in the Night

Mechanical Monster

This is a dream that Steve had when we were facing financial difficulties.

"I heard there was a mechanical fire-breathing monster destroying the town. Dianne and I got into our blue car to check it out. As we approached, the monster saw us and started to chase us. I was able to keep ahead of it but found I was approaching a 'T' intersection. A school was on one corner and a church on the other. Snow made the road slippery, but if I slowed down to make a turn in either direction, the monster would catch us. I stopped the car, walked into the middle of the road, and yelled 'JESUS!' The monster stopped in its tracks and said, 'Why didn't you say that earlier?' It then turned and walked away."

While reviewing our financial future, we were trying to decide if I should leave my full time ministry and take a secular job—back into mechanical engineering and design. We both felt the ministry was important, but we could not ignore our financial problems. This dream illustrated the crossroads we faced, deciding where to turn. As a solution, it offered us a different option. God was telling us to stop trying to struggle through in our own strength, face our spiritual enemy, the devourer, and in the name of Jesus send him running. The option we had been looking at—that of returning to secular employment—was slippery and dangerous.

No Backing Up

This is another dream Steve had.

"I was in a factory and went into the area where I used to work. A worker came to me, pointing out a flaw on a returned automotive part. There was evidence of overheating. I told him I would deliver the part to those in the office.

I found a company pickup truck and started to drive to the office. On the way there, some transport trailers were blocking the way. I started to back up, trying to go another way. At one point, a trailer that was backing up knocked off the driver's side rearview mirror on my truck. The jolt knocked the windshield mirror off as well. I was considering my next move when I woke up."

As with the preceding dream, Dianne and I had been asking the Lord whether I should augment our income with secular employment since things seemed to have slowed down in the ministries I was involved in. This dream indicated to me that God did not want me backing up. With the rearview mirrors gone, all I could safely do was go forward. This dream came to confirm the first.

Crime Scene

"I was a forensic detective on a crime scene. It was winter and we were investigating a fire. Someone had used a fuel as an accelerant to try to start two fires in one room. I found some paper matchsticks and fingerprints as evidence. Two regular police officers made fun of me while they were tampering with the evidence. A senior, more experienced forensic detective asked me when the fingerprint team would be arriving. I said I didn't know because no one had asked me to call them."

The evening before I (Steve) had this dream, I had had dinner with some friends. During the course of the evening, I had made a comment that I intended to be funny. Later that evening, it occurred to me that my friends could have taken my comment the wrong way and been hurt by it. I found myself overcome with remorse and began deriding myself. I went to bed troubled by those thoughts, and eventually fell asleep to that dream.

Counseled in the Night

The dream showed me that a perpetrator had tried to start a fire in my life. The senior detective (God) was drawing my attention to the fingerprints, because with those prints I could learn who had used the accelerant. My comment was innocent, but the perpetrator, a demonic influence, had used it to enflame self-pity and unwarranted remorse within me. This perpetrator had in effect ruined the remainder of my evening and attempted to destroy my joy. In the dream, God drew my attention off me and onto the perpetrator whose fingerprints and handiwork were evident in this situation. Through God's loving use of this dream, I was able to place this incident behind me and return to joy.

Download

The following dream offered counsel and direction that helped me (Steve) greatly in our ministry work.

"I was part of an underground resistance organization, and I had information that I needed to download to them. I went to one secret place to do that and as they were wiring me up for the download and touching the bare ends of two wires together, we realized that the enemy had discovered our location. They were coming and I had only a few minutes to escape before they arrived. As I was rushing out, someone handed me a bag of supplies.

"In the next scene, I was going to another location to attempt a download. Again, as they touched the bare ends of two wires together, we knew something had compromised our location. This time they were on us right away. I ran into a closet and the enemy stood there with his back to me. I thought I was a goner when someone handed me the bag of supplies and pointed to the front door. I ran out and down the street.

"As I ran, it occurred to me that my escape had been very costly to those who held back the enemy. After I ran for a few blocks, I started wondering if I should go down a side street, but then I noticed two of the enemy coming toward me on the sidewalk. I was behind a tree with my bright red coat, thinking I should have been wearing something less colorful. Just as the enemy saw me, I swung the bag of supplies and knocked them over and started to run again."

Strange dream, I thought as I pondered it. What could it possibly mean? I was having difficulty understanding the message, so I laid it aside, expecting more revelation to come later.

About two weeks later, I was on a train crossing the border into the United States. A Christian counseling center had invited me to teach a two-day seminar on God's Counsel and Healing through Dreams. I grew up in a border city and so crossing the border was nothing unusual for me—I had done it many times. I thought my documentation and invitation were in order, so I was not concerned about any difficulties.

That changed quickly when a U.S. Customs officer pulled me off the train and denied me entry into the country, saying that my documentation was incomplete. As I waited in the Customs office in disbelief, this dream suddenly came into my mind and I pondered its meaning relative to this new context. My wonderful wife drove two hours to pick up her forlorn husband at the border. In the dream, she represented the supplies handed to me as I escaped. Fortunately, the seminar organizers were able to cancel the seminar without incurring a great expense. The Customs officer had prevented me from downloading information to those who needed it at the seminar.

As I reflected on this, I realized that there would be a second attempt to download. Four weeks later I was supposed to fly to Australia to teach several seminars. It occurred to me that in the dream, the enemy caught us whenever we tried to touch the wires together. Could these wires represent "loose ends" in my paperwork?

Because of that dream, I began to pray more specifically about the trip to Australia. I worked with the travel agent to ensure that I had the proper paperwork and permits. That trip, for the purposes of "downloading information," was successful. Unlike a train ticket, if I had been refused entry into Australia, just the cost of the airfare could have been a huge setback. I wondered what knocking down two of the enemy officers might have represented. Thanks to God's message of direction in the dream, my trip to Australia was a success, and I did not need to know. God's counsel was of tremendous value to me.

Comfort

"I was in a classroom, teaching children. My husband appeared at the door. He came in and handed me my blanket. I was thrilled, and thought I would introduce him to the children."

The woman who shared this dream was excited about the meaning that was obvious to her the next morning. In the middle of the night, menstrual cramps had awakened her and she took some medication. Almost two hours later the pain was still keeping her awake and she considered taking a second dose. Instead, she fell asleep and had this dream. When she awoke, she realized that her husband represented Jesus. He had brought her the blanket, which represented comfort to her. She had slept and woke refreshed and ready for work.

Guidance

A pastor recounted the following dream.

"I was with a group at Disney World and met with Paul (a well known musician), his wife, and another lady, Joanne. Paul and his wife had a drinking problem. They were supposed to perform, but they were unable to because they were drunk. Paul's daughter (dark and shadowy in the dream) ran away with Joanne's daughter to a club ahead of us.

"I tried to catch them but then thought, "I'll stop and do it right." So I went back, picked up my wallet, organizer, and gym bag, and before rejoining the group. I took another route, a short cut, through the underground to the subterranean Disney city. I had no ID badge and walked with a limp. I came to a theatre room of employees in a training session where I ran up the aisles and did a comedy routine. Because I did so well, they promoted me and I went to another room.

"Meanwhile, Paul had just hit a '72 Chevelle driven by an old man, who was now faking an injury to get money. I told Paul to pay him $7500. The old man had a pink cat that slept all the time. As we walked, with Paul driving beside us, the two daughters came back. Paul's daughter explained what had happened."

The pastor asked me for help in understanding this personal dream. Disney World was a personal symbol to him of the kingdom of God—a fun place. He knew the woman who represented Paul's wife by her features in the dream. This helped us determine that Paul might represent a friend who was a musician and worship leader. The pastor had recently become aware that this couple had a drinking problem that was getting out of control. He had tried to per-

Counseled in the Night

suade them to stop, but concluded that he should take a different approach.

The dream told him that he needed to go to them with his wallet—his identity as a friend; his organizer—a plan and a routine; and his gym bag—leisure activities. These would help them find the root of the problem, which was represented by the daughters of the worship leader and Joanne. Paul's daughter, being dark and shadowy, may have indicated demonic activity associated with their problem. Armed with his wallet, organizer, and gym bag, the pastor needed to look below the surface to find the problem. Even though he had no ID badge—credentials as a counselor—and limped, which indicated he felt ill equipped, he would be successful because of what he did have—himself.

Hitting the old man in the '72 Chevelle (the dreamer's first car), referred to a hope that the pastor had that Paul, who was well off, might support his ministry if the pastor helped him. This came from the pastor's old self or sinful nature. The return of the daughters represented a resolution of the issue.

The dream gave the pastor the confidence to approach his friend about these issues.

Eagle's Flight

Another dream from a pastor:

"I was part of the swim team with others there. We were doing the backstroke. Then I was at a singles' dance with other people, and they were trying to set me up with someone. I felt uncomfortable with that. Then I was water skiing. I saw two monsters under the surface of the water. One was a kid monster and the other a mother monster. I took my "James Bond" harpoon gun and shot them both, killing them. Then I took off like an eagle soaring in the sky. It felt wonderful."

The pastor told me this dream as we began a prayer ministry appointment. From a previous appointment, we knew there were still two memories that needed to be resolved. As we started, the Lord took him to a memory when, as a young boy of about three years old, he desperately wanted some of the cookies his mother was baking. To get his mother's attention, he was tugging at her apron. She was not responding and his tugging became frantic. Finally, she pushed him away.

Anger and resentment rose up in him to the point that he dissociated that memory and buried it deep in his subconscious. There it remained, affecting his life in subtle ways. By acknowledging that memory again, and in prayer asking forgiveness for the things he had done and extending forgiveness to his mother, he received healing and deliverance.

The second memory that the Lord brought to his attention was when as a small boy of five or six years old, he was on a picnic with his parents. At the playground he was on a teeter-totter with a smaller boy. The boy jumped off, causing him to crash to the ground and hurt himself. He was angry with the boy and wanted to hurt him, but his parents would not allow it. His anger and rage grew as he stormed around, trying to exact revenge from the boy.

He also hid this memory in his subconscious, dissociating himself from it. However, it was subconsciously affecting his relationships and robbing him of joy and peace. Again, he acknowledged his poor behavior, confessed his sin, and received healing and deliverance. Peace and joy were returning.

When we finished our appointment, I pointed out that

Counseled in the Night

his dream referred to a kid monster and a mother monster under the surface of the water—the subconscious. The two memories involved incidences with his mother and another child. The monsters in the dream were not these people in real life, but the memories and his responses to them.

Through this dream, the Lord was confirming the work he had done for the pastor that day. The backstroke swim and the singles dance related to relationship problems stemming from these two memories. The exciting part was the anticipated flight—like an eagle—that would follow. Overall, the dream confirmed the work completed during the prayer ministry appointment. It left him with the expectation of an eagle's flight, a release from the things that had been holding him down.

Waiting Rooms

"I was in a waiting area with a couple of other people, waiting to go into another room to prophesy over people. I noticed the closed door to the room I was to enter."

This woman had been discovering a prophetic gifting. She had also displayed insights and understanding in the interpretation of dreams and visions. In another dream, she was even "called by my (Steve's) office," which to her represented a calling to dream interpretation. Being anxious to exercise this gift, she began to ask the Lord for his leading. Through this waiting room dream, the Lord was asking her to wait until he "opened the door."

She also had another dream where she was in an airport. She had passed through the checkpoint and was in the departure lounge. While there, she received her grade mark for a course she was taking for her Master's degree. It was lower than she had hoped, but the professor noted that she had more work to do that would help her grade. Here too, God had her in a time of waiting, asking her to do some more work.

In both cases, she was pleased not only to wait, but also to receive instruction from the Lord. During this waiting period, she determined to learn all she could about these spiritual gifts.

Missed the Plane

"I was in an airport and distracted by various things around me. By the time I got to the departure gate, ticket in hand, my plane had left. I missed my plane."

This woman woke up from the dream feeling as if she was a failure; making mistakes and missing opportunities. The context of her life was that in her church she had taken many training courses. She hoped these would afford her a chance to participate in a ministry or as part of a prophetic team. However, because of distractions in her life, she had never made the necessary commitment.

The dream spoke to her regarding this problem. She is well trained—at the airport ready to fly—but she got distracted and only managed to get to the gate. She missed her plane. It was time to start catching the plane.

This dream produced fear and condemnation until the woman understood the message. Then her countenance changed and she became excited about the future, feeling that others needed her gifts and maybe she did have something to contribute. Her parting remark to me was, "There has been healing for me today!"

Conclusions

Counsel can be defined as advice or guidance given,

Counseled in the Night

usually by someone with greater understanding.

God's counsel is not limited to leaders of large organizations, although it is often important for them. Everyone needs his counsel. We may only be "leading" one or two family members, but the family unit, is one of the cornerstones of larger communities. To help, God has given us the Holy Spirit who will give us needed guidance and counsel.

> "But when He, the Spirit of truth, comes, He will guide you into all the truth; for He will not speak on His own initiative, but whatever He hears, He will speak; and He will disclose to you what is to come. He will glorify Me, for He will take of Mine and will disclose it to you. All things that the Father has are Mine; therefore I said that He takes of Mine and will disclose it to you" (John 16:13–15).

Through many wonderful and creative ways, God has been able to give counsel to his people and reveal things about their future that has helped them. Pastor Robert's declaration sums it up well: "I would not want to be in the ministry without dreams to help me. Yes, they're important to me."

God has a plan for our lives. He will help us to walk in that plan if we are willing. There may be times that we are not willing; times when unknown fears hold us back. Behind these fears, there may be emotional issues or related memories that require healing. Any or all of these may act as barriers to an abundant life, fullness of joy, and peace. These issues need God's healing and his sanctifying work and as we have seen, it can often come through dreams.

Steve & Dianne Bydeley

8 Sanctification

God has a very important objective in the lives of believers—that we become more like Jesus.[28] This means that we increasingly love God far more than we love ourselves and that we love our neighbors as much as we do ourselves.[29] Theologians often refer to this process of becoming like Jesus as the process of sanctification, of becoming saintly, or of becoming holy.

This chapter explains some basic principles of the process of sanctification. We believe it is important to have a clear understanding of it before we explore how God speaks to us about this through dreams. Experience has shown us that those who do not are often plagued by feelings of condemnation, hopelessness, and despair.

> "For those whom He foreknew, He also predestined to become conformed to the image of His Son, so that He would be the firstborn among many brethren; and these whom He predestined, He also called; and these whom He called, He also justified; and these whom He justi-

fied, He also glorified" (Romans 8:29–30).

As we mentioned in Chapter 6, about 90–95 percent of our dreams are personal—dreams that are for and about the dreamer. When we combine this finding with the concept that God wants us to change and become more like Jesus, we have the essence of many of the messages of our dreams. God uses dreams to reveal what he is doing in our lives or to show us what we need to surrender to him in order to be sanctified.

The process of sanctification is cooperative and interactive in that it requires our willingness, our consent—our participation. This can be an obstacle if we are not convinced that we want the qualities of Jesus' character to be our own. Our culture has many deeply imbedded values and customs that are at odds with Jesus. For example, western society largely views meekness and humility as signs of weakness. This may inhibit us from bringing these Christ like qualities into our lives.

So we may have to ask ourselves, "Is being strong and in control important to me, or do I really see gentleness and submission to God as qualities I should pursue with determination?" Not only do we need to look honestly into our hearts, we need a clear understanding of the process of sanctification so that we can interpret many of the dreams we dream.

The Process of Sanctification

"As obedient children, do not be conformed to the former lusts which were yours in your ignorance, but like the Holy One who called you, be holy yourselves also in all your behavior; because it is written, 'YOU SHALL BE HOLY, FOR I AM HOLY'" (1 Peter 1:14–16).

Sanctified

Not only is holiness God's plan for us subsequent to salvation, he has predestined, or predetermined, that this will take place during the remainder of our life on earth and/or when we are transformed on Christ's return.[30] In Paul's Epistle to the Ephesians, he tells us that we are God's workmanship.[31] He is the craftsman and we are the objects of his craft. He is the potter and we are the clay.[32]

At this point, many believers comment, "When I gave my life to Christ, I thought that from that point on, God only saw in me the righteousness of Christ?" This is a valid observation and one to which we need to add clarity. While our salvation is assured, the verses from Romans 8 make it clear that there is a separate process through which we become like Jesus. Concerning this, Paul writes:

> "Now may the God of peace Himself sanctify you entirely; and may your spirit and soul and body be preserved complete, without blame at the coming of our Lord Jesus Christ. Faithful is He who calls you, and He also will bring it to pass" (1 Thessalonians 5:23–24).

God will sanctify us entirely; he will bring it to pass. In this passage, Paul identifies three distinct units of our being: the spirit, soul, and body. By understanding the interplay between these parts and God's plan of salvation, we gain valuable insights into our Christian life and our relationship with the Father. To do this, let's go back to where it all started, to the roots.

Rooted in the Garden

In the first chapter of Genesis God said, "Let Us make man in Our image, according to Our likeness" (v.26).

What does God's likeness or image represent? Is it related to their Trinitarian nature—Father, Son, and Holy Spirit—and our nature; spirit, soul, and body? No one knows for sure, but this is a possible explanation or a part of it. When Adam and his wife (not named Eve until after the fall) disobeyed God's command by eating the fruit of the tree of the knowledge of good and evil, they died just as God had said they would.[33] How are we to understand that death?

> "Then the eyes of both of them were opened, and they knew that they were naked; . . . and the man and his wife hid themselves from the presence of the LORD God among the trees of the garden" (Genesis 3:7–8).

That act of disobedience affected their spirit, soul, and body. We can read the consequences in the third chapter of Genesis 3—their eyes were opened (soul or mind), they realized their nakedness (body), and they hid from God (spiritually separated). These three phrases, brief as they were, have deeply influenced the billions of people who have lived since then. These influences include the overwhelming need for healing—the removal of the wounds that sin and hurt have left in us.

In the same way, the obedience of the last Adam, Jesus, has affected, for our salvation, these three areas of our being.[34] In our place he was forsaken by the Father (spirit),[35] held captive and tortured (soul),[36] and was crucified (body), so that we would no longer have to be influenced by the first Adam's disobedience.

Our Spirit

> "Now there was a man of the Pharisees, named Nicodemus, a ruler of the Jews; this man came to Jesus by night and said to Him, 'Rabbi, we know that You have come from God as a teacher; for no one can do these signs that You do unless God is with him.'
>
> "Jesus answered and said to him, 'Truly, truly, I say to you, unless one is born again he cannot see the kingdom

of God.' Nicodemus said to Him, 'How can a man be born when he is old? He cannot enter a second time into his mother's womb and be born, can he?'

"Jesus answered, 'Truly, truly, I say to you, unless one is born of water and the Spirit he cannot enter into the kingdom of God. That which is born of the flesh is flesh, and that which is born of the Spirit is spirit. Do not be amazed that I said to you, "You must be born again"'" (John 3:3–7).

Jesus clearly emphasizes the importance of being "born again" as a prerequisite to seeing the kingdom of God. What occurs when we are born again? Jesus connects rebirth with the Spirit. "That which is born of the flesh is flesh, and that which is born of the Spirit is spirit."

When we receive the gift of salvation from God, bought and paid for by the life, death, and resurrection of Jesus Christ, our spirits are born again, or born anew, by the Holy Spirit. At that point, Jesus saves us from damnation and brings us into relationship with the Father.

Our Soul

We understand the soul to entail our minds, wills, and emotions. Aside from spiritual death, it is the soul that has been tainted by sin. The Bible refers to this as the sinful nature, the former self.[37] Until our spirits are reborn, each of us lives our lives in our human nature. The soul requires sanctifying or inner healing from the emotional and spiritual wounds that act as barriers to a life of joy and peace. Once someone receives Christ into his heart and yields his will, God begins to transform his soul into the image of Christ, healing the mind and emotions. It is to the soul that God's counsel comes in dreams as he works in us.

God accomplishes most of this transformational healing, but the process is interactive. God will not force change onto us. He expects that we will be motivated by a love for him to surrender any unrighteousness that he reveals in us. As he progressively sanctifies us, we become more like Jesus in our character and nature.

Our Body

The body is our "earth suit"—the part of us that enables us to live on earth. This earth suit is the container, the "earthen vessel"[38] that houses our spirit and soul. We have a responsibility to take proper care of it until we die. Our bodies often display the effects of emotional and spiritual wounds in our soul. On Jesus' return, he will eliminate these as well. Paul writes: "So also is the resurrection of the dead. It is sown a perishable body, it is raised an imperishable body" (1 Corinthians 15:42). This resurrection, the redemption of our bodies, is a future event, and one we look forward to when the trumpet sounds.

The Work of the Cross

Jesus' crucifixion, spiritual separation from God, the suffering of his soul, and the death of his body addressed each of the areas affected by the disobedience of Adam. The first Adam created the problem and the second Adam, Jesus, resolved it. Just as we inherited the consequences of Adam's disobedience, so too, we inherit the consequences of Jesus' obedience. Adam chose to eat the fruit from a live tree in Eden and died. We can partake of the fruit of Jesus' death on a dead tree at Golgotha and live.

Jesus' work on the cross restores us to a right relationship with the Father. It is not possible to overemphasize how much Jesus' suffering, death, and resurrection accomplished for us. Those acts of love had ramifications that every believer will spend an eternity appreciating. Jesus died so that we could live an abundant life and enter into his joy, healing, and wholeness.

Conclusion

This work of making us more Christ-like is the process of sanctification and pertains mainly to the soul part of the three areas of our nature—spirit, soul, and body. We have seen how Jesus' work on the cross has addressed each of these areas so that we now have confidence to approach the throne of grace. We see that when we receive God's gift of salvation, he makes our spirits alive by his Spirit. His Spirit in us is our guarantee that we have a place with him, regardless of where we are in the process of becoming like Jesus.

At the time of our salvation, our soul entered into a process of sanctification wherein God began to transform us into the image of Jesus. He will complete this process when we see him. As Paul writes, "For I am confident of this very thing, that He who began a good work in you will perfect it until the day of Christ Jesus" (Philippians 1:6). Finally, we know that when Jesus returns, He will give us new bodies, a heaven suit—imperishable.

In summary then, we are completely saved (our spirit), we are being saved (our soul), and we will be saved (our bodies). So then, what does our sanctification have to do with inner healing or with dreams?

If after reading this, you realize that you have not yet entered into this wonderful relationship with the Father, please seriously consider it. If you would like to do so now, please read the following prayer. If this is what you want to experience and enjoy, then repeat it again, preferably aloud:

Lord Jesus, I have sinned in the past and expect I will sin in the future.[39] I understand that these sins, and my tendency to sin, separate me from relationship with you.[40] I understand that you died on the cross, paying the price for the sin[41] of all who will believe this, so that we can stand before God in your perfection. [42] It is my desire to receive your payment for my past, present, and future sin, so please be the payment for all my sin.

Lord, from this moment on, all my sin has been paid for and nothing now separates me from being in relationship with you—I thank you.[43] Lord, please fill me with your Holy Spirit,[44] teach me the details of what has just happened to me, and especially teach me to grow in my new relationship with you.[45] Thank you, Jesus; I look forward to getting to know you.

If you prayed this prayer, please tell someone that you have made this decision to be in close relationship to Jesus.[46]

9 Inner Healing

In this chapter we take a look at a deeper form of sanctification known as inner healing. Understanding the principals of inner healing helps greatly in interpreting the messages of our dreams.

Jesus began his public ministry when he read from the scripture in the synagogue at Nazareth. It was customary for the synagogue ruler to select a male adult to read, and on this occasion he chose Jesus, giving him a scroll of scripture from the book of Isaiah. Jesus read from the sixty-first chapter:

> "'The Spirit of the Lord is on me, because he has anointed me to preach good news to the poor. He has sent me to proclaim freedom for the prisoners and recovery of sight for the blind, to release the oppressed, to proclaim the year of the Lord's favor.' Then he rolled up the scroll, gave it back to the attendant and sat down. The eyes of everyone in the synagogue were fastened on him, and he began by saying to them, 'Today this scripture is fulfilled in your hearing'" (Luke 4:18-21 NIV).

The words of Isaiah that Jesus read speak of healing and freedom for the prisoners and the oppressed. The verses define what inner healing is, what it does, and who does it-Jesus. Inner healing is ultimately about Jesus, the "Wonderful Counselor" of Isaiah.[47]

Inner healing is a relatively new term and we frequently receive blank expressions when we mention it as a Christian ministry. Other terms have been used to describe it, including: the healing of memories, Prayer Healing,[48] Listening Prayer,[49] Healing Prayer,[50] Prayer Counseling,[51] and TheoPhostic[52] counseling. Each of these terms may represent differences in various aspects of the counseling, but the essence of each approach is the same—Jesus setting the prisoners free.

John Sandford of Elijah House Prayer Ministry[53] identifies four scriptural principles that form the foundation for inner healing.

- Honor your parents so that you will live long and do well[54]
- When you judge others, you bring judgment upon yourself[55]
- You reap what you sow[56]
- When you judge someone, you condemn yourself[57]

Some others include:

- Refusing to forgive someone[58]
- Sins of the fathers (ancestral sin)[59]
- Ungodly beliefs rooted in childhood[60]

Many people are not aware of these issues or influences in their lives. This can present a major obstacle to inner healing. Often they have been buried or hidden, consciously or unconsciously, in the past. However, they still

Inner Healing

affect us and we are responsible for them. Our legalistic enemy, the demonic realm, will try to use any unresolved sin in our lives to hinder us.

Marked at Birth

A middle-aged woman came to us seeking prayer. She told us that she had harbored feelings of rejection and inadequacy for most of her life. She was quite personable, and while considering her history we could not account for these feelings. Was she to live the rest of her life in this condition—always feeling rejected, always lacking the fullness of joy and abundant life that Jesus came to give us? Were there no answers, no solutions—no hope?

In our discussions and prayer, God revealed to this woman that she had been born with a birth defect, a large red blemish in the middle of her forehead. Her mother subsequently confirmed this, saying that it had eventually disappeared and she had forgotten about it. Suddenly things started to come together. As a newborn baby, this woman had felt, heard, and seen her parents' first reaction to this blemish and interpreted their dismay as being their disappointment of her. When family members and friends first saw her, their negative reactions reinforced these impressions.

Having discovered the root cause of her problems, the woman could now forgive those who unknowingly contributed to her feelings of rejection. Jesus subsequently told her, during listening prayer, how much he loved her as a tiny baby, and that her parents had always loved and accepted her. He explained that their disappointment concerned the birthmark, not her. This all brought tears of joy. She asked and received forgiveness for her wrong conclusion. This enabled her to receive healing and finally be free of feelings of rejection She was finally free from the bondage.

Unless God had revealed the root cause of her problems, it may have been impossible to identify them and subsequently bring Jesus' healing words into her life.

Definition

As a result of our experience, we have developed a working definition of inner healing.

> Inner healing is the miraculous application of forgiveness and truth, by Jesus, to sin and misunderstandings rooted in the wounds of our memories. It frees us from present emotional and physical problems.

This definition could almost be applied to the gift of salvation and sanctification as well. The Greek words for saved, healed, whole, are the same word—sozo. The difference between inner healing and sanctification relate to the differences between the spirit and the soul. When by faith we choose to receive the gift of salvation based on the sinless life, death, and bodily resurrection of Jesus, his sacrifice is our salvation. At that time, our souls begin the sanctification process.

While he was with us on earth, Jesus inaugurated the coming of the kingdom of God. When he returns, he will consummate it. In the meantime we live in the tension of "the already but not yet." Jesus' work is already finished, but not yet completed. It is on the aspect of the "not yet," or the sanctification of our souls (our mind, will, and emotions), that we will focus our attention.

After receiving salvation, everyone soon faces the conflict depicted in Romans 7—the struggle between the desire of our spirit to please God and that of our flesh to live selfishly. Pleasing God relates to loving God above all else and loving our neighbors as ourselves. This is an issue of

Inner Healing

relationship, not of salvation. We are already saved. Were we to die seconds after receiving the gift of salvation, we have God's declaration in writing that we will be with him in heaven forever.[61]

However, until the time of our death, we struggle with the inclination to do wrong—to be selfish. During this period, from our salvation until our natural death, we are in the process of sanctification. This is also called the renewing of our minds[62] or putting on the new self.[63] God has promised to complete this process of sanctification in us by his Holy Spirit. He has taken responsibility for that task.

As we have said before, sanctification is a cooperative, interactive process. We must participate. As we yield the selfish or unloving areas of our lives to God, he is able to sanctify us, to change us. If we choose not to yield an area to him,[64] then we continue to suffer the consequences until our death, when God will change us instantly into the image of his Son. Until we die, he chooses to honor our will.

Why would we not eagerly invite Jesus into every area of our lives, since he has so wonderfully demonstrated his love for us? Sadly, there are many reasons.

Triggering a Root Memory

Jesus had many things to say about relationship, as does most of the Bible. Periodically we have conflict in relationships and when we do, we often have difficulty identifying who has the problem. Jesus talked about this:

> "Why do you look at the speck that is in your brother's eye, but do not notice the log that is in your own eye? Or how can you say to your brother, 'Let me take the speck out of your eye,' and behold, the log is in your own eye? You hypocrite, first take the log out of your own eye, and then you will see clearly to take the speck

out of your brother's eye" (Matthew 7:3–5).

The problem is often one of specks and logs. God created us for relationship. As adult believers, that relationship is to be with God, our spouse, our children, and with others, in that order.[65] Satan's first and most effective attack against God has been to damage our capacity for relationship. When sin came, Adam and Eve hid themselves from God and from each other. In reading the third chapter of Genesis we see the immediate effect of this damage in their newfound ability to blame each other for their problem.

How does this blaming show itself in the text from the Gospel of Matthew? As specks and logs! The effects of sin in our world and in the lives of every human being result in wounds that we inflict and receive. These primary wounds often remain deeply rooted until Jesus heals them. As long as they are not healed, they can act as triggers, waiting for someone or something to touch them.

Think of them as a gun. When you pull the trigger of a loaded gun, the result is a lot of noise and a bullet leaves the gun, hitting whatever is in front of it. The key to finding the trigger is not to follow the bullet, but to find the source of the noise. The noise not only tells us that someone pulled a trigger, it will also lead us to the one who owns the trigger—the primary wound. The one who makes all the noise about another person is often the one who owns the originating problem.

In the life of a child, many negative life experiences can act as triggers. These include: premature birth, adoption, marriage problems of the parents, abandonment, sexual/physical abuse, and financial hardships. The trauma or wrong conclusions a child may come to about these events can become the roots of deep-seated memories,

Inner Healing

which in turn become the belief structures that affect their lives and relationships into adulthood.

When a negative event occurs in an adult relationship, that event often triggers a reaction based on the emotions of a similar childhood root memory. In other words, the negative event triggers the brain to sort through a database of past events to find an event that is similar to the present one. When the brain finds a close match, it re-enacts the emotions of that childhood match in the current situation. Here are some examples.

Golf

A husband and wife are arguing. The wife is angry because the husband wants to play a round of golf with some friends. Her complaint is that he is leaving her alone and she does not want to be alone—again. He is angry because he is usually with her and he doesn't play golf often. Who has the speck and who has the log? Can you judge between these two? Do you know all the facts? Let us look deeper.

Imagine this woman as a four-year-old girl. Her father was a traveling salesperson and needed to be away from home to earn a living. She was hurt when the most significant man in her life left her at home—alone. Oh yes, mother was home, but that little girl wanted and needed her father's attention. She felt rejected. She thought, "If he really loved me, he would stay." This was not true of course, but her young mind cannot think logically and she believed it to be true. She wanted and needed him to validate her, but he was always leaving.

The girl/woman's misunderstanding of her father's responsibilities, and to some degree her father's insensitivity to her needs, caused the hurt she felt as a little girl. This is not a case of passing blame onto the father. Regardless of whether he was right or wrong in his actions, it is her response to his actions, her judgment, for which she is accountable. The girl's brain records the emotions of that scenario into her memory and there it remains as a trigger. Later in life, anything that closely resembles that original event will cause her to experience those same emotions.

Back to the future. The golfer husband is leaving for that morning round of golf. This triggers that childhood hurt in his wife's heart. She responds with emotional outbursts of criticism that wound her husband. An argument is started that cannot be resolved without one or both of them being hurt.

Who has the speck and who has the log?

Enter Jesus, the Wonderful Counselor of Isaiah.[66] He is able to bring healing to the hurts at the point in the past when they entered the heart of the little girl. He can do this because he is not subject to time as are we. He brings the light of his truth to dispel the dark misunderstandings in the memories of the little girl. During prayer ministry[67] Jesus affirms her. He tells her that she is precious, that she is never alone—he is with her. As she confesses her misunderstandings and expresses forgiveness to her father for the hurt that his actions caused, Jesus removes the trigger and brings healing to that memory. Instead of emotions, pain, and hurt, that memory now carries the truth that Jesus spoke to the little girl.

Enter the golfer a few weeks later. This time his departure can find no trigger; in fact, his wife sees his absence as opportunity to pursue some of her interests. The husband and wife bless each other as they part and look forward to being together later.

This same scenario could involve sexual and/or physical abuse in the life of a child. Many times the adult has no memory of that abuse, because the child has buried it, or lacks understanding in the ways that abuse affects their relationships as an adult. These primary wounds remain, often hidden, as the roots that produce bad fruit later in life.

Scolding

While at work, John's supervisor scolds him for an oversight. This has happened once or twice before, without any problem. This time, sudden feelings of fear drive John to panic, surprising his supervisor. What happened?

Perhaps the way the supervisor shook his finger this time as he spoke was similar to an event in John's youth. An angry father shook his finger and then in a fit of rage, punished him excessively. John's brain might have stored that childhood experience as an emotional event. The similarity to the supervisor's actions is close enough that John's brain presented him with the painful emotional experience of that childhood event.

John's adult response to his supervisor may have seemed irrational to others, but not necessarily to John. The trigger influences of past wounds often cause us to react seemingly irrationally in similar present-day situations. We may lash out against the one "hurting" us, wounding them and damaging relationships. And so the destructive cycle continues until Jesus removes the root that triggers that wound.

Roots

The quality of the fruit of the plant always reflects the quality of the root of the plant. Bad fruit means a bad root![68]

Many homeowners in North America are aware of the dandelion dilemma. No matter how often you mow the lawn, cutting the yellow flowers, dandelions continue to reappear. The only way to get rid of the weed is to tediously dig up the root. Where there is no root there is no dandelion. In our spiritual lives, roots produce fruit that manifest themselves in many ways, all affecting our relationships and our lives.

It is through relationships, especially when we are young, that people can wound us emotionally. This occurs when we may, with our immature minds, wrongly interpret the actions of others around us, or respond in wrong ways. For example, it is common for abused children to blame themselves for causing the event. They assume they did something to attract the abuse, and therefore they are bad. Or the child may hold anger, bitterness, resentment, unforgiveness, etc. toward the abuser. Although we can understand why they would have these emotions, we are never justified in holding onto them.[69]

Perhaps a child senses or overhears that her birth was the cause of the family's financial hardships, leading her to believe the family would be better off without her. Alternatively, if a playmate rejects a child, he may believe that no one will ever like him. Regardless of what others may have done to us, we are accountable for our response to their actions! It does not matter what the wrong was, if we do not forgive others, God will not forgive us.[70] This is a law as real as the law of gravity.

Rejection

In my own life, I (Steve) was often depressed and felt rejected by others and never knew why. As I studied inner

Inner Healing

healing issues, it occurred to me that as child number nine of ten, my parents were probably not thrilled with my conception (cute as I was). I also learned that my mother had a difficult pregnancy with number eight sibling, which could have added to her lack of enthusiasm.

From an adult's perspective, my parent's reaction is understandable—logical. Not so for an infant. As an infant, or perhaps even as a fetus, I sensed my parents' reluctance and eventually, as a child, concluded that I was not wanted. My problem was not my parent's attitude; it was my judgment of them and the negative conclusion I came to—my response.

These conclusions were traumatic at that early age so I hid them in my memory, hoping that they would somehow go away so that I would never to have to deal with them. However, they unconsciously remained active, causing me to expect everyone to reject me—until Jesus, Wonderful Counselor, healed my wound. In my mind, as a logical adult, I know that my parents did not reject me. I know they loved me when I was born, but as a child I believed I was not wanted. That child in me needed to hear the truth. Only Jesus can speak that truth into the heart of the child, because yesterday, tomorrow, and today are all "now" to him. His truth set me free.

In prayer ministry sessions, we ask Jesus to take a client into the memory that holds the root cause of the problem. We do not suggest a memory to the client, nor do we ask her to visualize a contrived, made-up situation. Both of these actions are inappropriate. We simply ask Jesus to take the client to the root memory as it actually occurred. Clients often say something to the effect of, "Wow, I forgot all about that," as Jesus calls a memory to their attention. We listen as they describe some long-forgotten event that actually occurred and see how it has been damaging to their relationships. We ask Jesus to speak his truth into that memory, removing the bad root. When this happens, the trigger is removed.

Memories and Dissociation

As we have seen, the left and right sides of our brain perform different functions. Our left side functions in logic, sequences, and chronological memories that are all subject to voluntary or conscious recall. Our right side functions in emotions, feelings, and creativity, which are involuntary or subconscious.

The prefrontal cortex of our right side also contains our "joy" center. When, as children, we experience events that are highly emotional and traumatic, our brains may choose not to store them in the left side, as part of our life history. Instead, because of their high emotional content, the events are stored in the right side of our brain. As a result, there is a gap in our life history where this memory would have been, and it is not subject to voluntary recall. The brain has dissociated the memory of that event from our active memory. We are then able to carry on with life in a relatively normal way, leaving the trauma for the adult to deal with later in life. This ability to dissociate seems to be a God-given mental safety valve.

The memory and emotions of these events remains hidden in the right side, among our other emotions, as a separated or dissociated memory. Often, as we reach our late thirties and early forties, these memories begin to "leak" their negative emotions, affecting our daily life, our relationships, and our joy center. Up to this point, we had the energy to suppress the emotions of the event but as we age, we lose that energy.

The result of this leakage—unexplained sadness, relationship and physical problems, uncontrolled emotions—drive many of us to medication, counseling, illegal drugs, various coping mechanisms, or God for healing. We experience the consequences of the leakage, but we are never quite sure what is going on. As we have seen, present events may trigger these hidden past memories, causing us to experience past pain in the present moment and sometimes hurting others through our apparent over-reaction.

Healing comes when we invite Jesus to reveal and heal the emotions of the memory, thereby allowing it to return to its proper position in our life history. The leaking stops and its influences on our lives are limited to that of any other historical event.

Conclusion

As in the Garden of Eden, we too resort to the blame game. Adam blamed God for the woman who caused his disobedience, Eve blamed God for creating the serpent that enticed her to sin, and the serpent smiled. The only route out of that dilemma is to accept responsibility for our sin rather than pass the blame. It is when we confess our sin that God is faithful and just to forgive and cleanse us. Stop the blame game. Take responsibility and be forgiven and cleansed.

Armed with a basic understanding of inner healing, wounds, triggers, and roots, we can now embark on the interpretation of dreams. God is more interested in our spiritual and emotional well-being than in our service or ministry.[72] Our dreams will reflect that interest by guiding and directing us to see and find these hidden issues and memories that act as barriers to our relationship with God and with those around us. Whether for our own dreams or for those we are helping, we are now better equipped to interpret dreams.

10   Healing Dream Symbols

Symbol: noun. "something that stands for or suggests something else by reason of relationship, association, convention, or accidental resemblance; especially : a visible sign of something invisible <the lion is a symbol of courage.>"[73]

The specialized symbols and meanings that we look at in this chapter are a guide to understanding how to use these and others in dreams that pertain to God's counsel and healing. We do not see these meanings as being definitive.

People versus Roles

People in dreams represent the greatest challenge in interpretation. There are three main categories of people in our dreams—relatives, people we know, and people that we do not know. Each of these categories plays a role in understanding the symbol. Relatives often represent a quality or aspect of the dreamer. Those we know but are not related to could represent some aspect of relationship or ministry, and those people who are strangers can represent anything else.

These are not hard and fast rules. We offer them as guidelines to assist you in understanding people as symbols.

One quite natural mistake that many people make is to assume that people we know in dreams represent themselves as they do in real life relationships. This assumption can result in misunderstanding, confusion and hurt, especially if we talk to those people about the dream.

In our personal experience, if someone tells us about a dream that he believes is for and about us because we are in the dream, we listen to his account of the dream. Then we determine the dreamer's role in the story. If it is active, we suggest that he examine the dream as a personal dream—one that is for and about him. We explain that our active role in their dream is symbolic of something that pertains to him; something that he needs to discover. In such a scenario, the people in the dream that the dreamer recognizes are acting out a role. This role is what is important to the message of the dream, not who they are in real life.

A comparison can be made to movie actors. In one movie, an actor may play a villain, while in another movie, a hero. We accept this discrepancy because we are accustomed to looking at the role that the actor is playing, not the actual actor. This is how we should see people in our dreams—look at the role rather than the person. Look at personal qualities and see if they are the same as the role they play in the dream.

Dianne and I once took acting lessons to help us (actually me) feel free to animate during our seminar presentations. During those lessons, we often had to assume the roles of different characters from one or two pages of a script and act out those roles with others. Our primary objective was to try to understand the characters, their background, how they fit into relationships, their demeanor, and their personality traits. Until we had a good grasp of those details, we could not enter into the roles with any degree of conviction. Those acting exercises helped us analyze the roles of people in our dreams and avoid getting entangled in the symbolism, all the while trying to uncover the message of the dream.

Relatives in Dreams

When people who are related to the dreamer appear in the dream, they often represent qualities or aspects of the dreamer to which God is drawing attention. The quality of relationship we have or had with that relative may also influence their representation.

Fathers

Someone has a personal dream and her father is in it. She should remind herself that this does not mean that the dream is for or about her father. It is for and about her.

She could ask herself if the father plays a leading role (aside from the dreamer of course), or does he have a secondary role. A primary role deserves more effort in trying to understand the symbol. God used the father as a symbol for a purpose, not because he ran out of characters.

In real life, what is the father's role in the life of the dreamer? Does he represent someone she loves, admires, and respects? Does she like to be with him, or is he feared, strict, difficult, or distant? Is he an authority figure in her life, or did he spoil her? When she thinks she has established his role or character from the perspective of her life, she needs to test it to see if it fits the role he played in the dream. The emotions she experienced in the dream often help to bring clarity to his meaning as a symbol.

Does he represent something outside of her, or some quality within her? For example, the father who she loved and respected could represent God the Father in her dream, giving her direction or correction. A father who was overly strict and who made life difficult would not represent God. It may represent her wrong perspective of God as her Father, if that needs correction, or it may represent a quality she has that came from her father.

A man once came to us for help in understanding a dream. The dream revealed that his father would die in September. As it was August, the man was understandably concerned. When we asked him what came to mind when he thought about his father, he used words like judgmental and controlling. Apparently his father was always putting him down for being unsuccessful. We then asked him what was happening in his life around the time of the dream. He shared how he had enrolled in school, upgrading his education in order to qualify for a better job.

We interpreted this dream to mean that, because of his schooling that was to begin in September, the effects of his father's scorn were going to die. In his dream, his father was symbolic of those negative traits that had taken root and were affecting his outlook on life. For others with a positive fatherly role in their personal background, God the Father could have played a primary role in their dream, giving advice, direction, or encouragement.

People whose fathers have played a negative role in their lives may find that their father in their dreams could represent those similar poor qualities that have become a part of their life. The message of the dream could be that God wants them to become aware of these same poor qualities so that, by surrendering them, God can begin to remove them, causing them to become more Christ-like.

These are only a few ways of seeing the role of a father in our dreams. Stay open to other possibilities that God may show you.

Mothers

The advice given for fathers largely applies to mothers. As a good role model, a mother in a dream could represent the nurturing aspect of the Holy Spirit as he comes along side to help and teach us the things we need to know.

I (Dianne) once dreamed that I was outside in a grassy area with a few trees. It was a beautiful day. My mom was there and I laid my head on her knee.

When I later thought about my mother, her characteristics of nurturing, caring, giving, loving and being attentive were foremost in my mind. In this dream, my mother represented the Holy Spirit, who also has these qualities. The dream left me feeling wonderfully peaceful and secure in my spirit. Remembering this dream always causes me to "purr" deep within and relax. This was a comforting dream.

If we have grown up with an abusive mother, she would not represent the Holy Spirit. Rather, she may represent those qualities in us such as bitterness and resentment. God's purpose in bringing these sins to our attention is not to condemn us, but he hopes that we will confess them and give him permission to remove them from our lives.

Children

Children in our dreams have a variety of roles. Let's begin by discussing personal dreams in which children appear as a symbol. Again, we must recognize that the dream is not about the child. This is sometimes difficult as we see children in our dreams and immediately begin to think with our heart rather than our head. If God wanted to give us a message about our children, and he may want to do so, it would come as an impersonal dream—one that is for and about others, specifically about our children. He may also use a caregiver's dream, something we discuss in Chapter 12.

In a personal dream, we have to ask ourselves: "What is the role of the child in the dream?" In prayer ministry, we continue to learn of the importance of this area. We pay particular attention to any mention of a child in a dream, especially when there is a reference or inference to their age. In real life, babies, represent something new and wonderful in the lives of new parents. As we mentioned in *Dream Dreams*,[74] they could symbolize some new ministry, gifting, or quality God the Father is developing or giving us.

New Born Dream

I (Dianne) had a dream wherein I had just delivered a baby. The doctor called my husband and me so that we could meet with him. As we approached him, I saw him sitting in a rather large and regal chair. He was older and looked very kind. I remembered that in the dream, I thought the baby was "9–2 (nine pounds, two ounces.)." But the doctor informed me it was "9–7." He then told me that he was going teach to me how to care for and nurture the baby.

In this dream, the baby represented a good thing, a new thing that the Father (the doctor) had brought into my life. The date of my wedding was 9/7. I understood this to mean that the Father was going to teach me how to care for and nurture my new marriage relationship.

The Dreamer's Children

Children we recognize in our dreams can represent ourselves at an earlier time in our lives—a time that may be significant to our well-being today.

No Diapers Dream

There was a scene in a dream where the dreamer happened upon an abandoned baby. The baby was lying on and soiling a mattress. The dreamer was trying to find diapers to care for the baby, but she could not locate any. The dream ended and she awoke in frustration.

When we asked questions about the early years of her life, she recounted that her parents had neglected her. In the dream, God was showing her that those events from her past, when she was a baby, were soiling her present relationships. With her cooperation, God wanted to bring healing and liberty into that area of her life.

Coffin Dream

In this dream a woman walked into a funeral parlor with her daughter, who seemed to be about three years old. As they entered, the woman approached a coffin and was shocked to see her fiancé lying inside.

The dream concerned her because she feared that her fiancé's life was in danger. I asked her what had happened to her when she was three years old. My question shocked her and she asked me how I knew. Someone had sexually abused her at that time. Her three-year-old daughter (who in real life is much older) represented the abuse of that period. Her fiancé represented her pending marriage. The coffin did not represent the death of the fiancé, but the potential end to the marriage. Through this dream, God was bringing those childhood events to her attention in the hope she would surrender them to him for healing. If left unresolved, they would harm her future marriage relationship.

Piano Dream

"I was sitting on the edge of a piano seat in the doorway to our kitchen. A little girl came from behind me with a toy cat that looked and sounded like a real one. When I turned around and saw it, I jumped. The little girl said, 'We really need you to get over your fear of cats, because I really want one as a pet.'"

When I asked the woman to tell me of her experiences with piano lessons, my question surprised her. She told of her many different teachers and the fear she experienced with some of them. Her family members expressed anger toward her during her practice times, which also made her fearful. The little girl in this dream represented issues of fear in her past that the Lord wanted to remove from her life.

Notice the words of the little girl, "We need you to get over your fear . . ." Because of allergies and other personal experiences regarding cats, they represent fear to this woman. This little girl represents a dissociate memory that needs the inner healing that only Jesus can provide.

Grandparents

As with fathers and mothers, a grandfather and grandmother can represent God the Father and the Holy Spirit respectively, if they have had a positive influence in the dreamer's life. As with parents, there are other ways of seeing grandparents, depending on the context of the symbol in the dream. They can often depict ancestral or generational problems, which are important to identify because they have an effect on our lives.[75]

I, the LORD your God, am a jealous God, visiting the

iniquity of the fathers on the children, on the third and the fourth generations of those who hate Me, but showing lovingkindness to thousands, to those who love Me and keep My commandments" (Exodus 20:5–6).

These verses tell us that the consequences of the sins of our fathers, or forefathers, can affect us in good or bad ways. God is willing to forgive these things and remove their effects in our lives through confession, which means, to acknowledge as wrong.

"If they confess their iniquity and the iniquity of their forefathers, in their unfaithfulness which they committed against Me, and also in their acting with hostility against Me—I also was acting with hostility against them, to bring them into the land of their enemies—or if their uncircumcised heart becomes humbled so that they then make amends for their iniquity, then I will remember My covenant with Jacob, and I will remember also My covenant with Isaac, and My covenant with Abraham as well, and I will remember the land" (Leviticus 26:40–42).

The solution seems simple enough—if we are aware of problems with our forefathers. The catch is in the knowing. In a more general sense, the sin of Adam our ancestor continues to affect us today. It is only when we acknowledge and confess that we are sinners that we can avail ourselves of God's gift of salvation. How can we respond if we know nothing of the activities of our more recent ancestors? How can we know if the things that plague us are attributable to them? God our Father often uses dreams to speak to us about issues like that—if we have an ear to hear him. God has a role in the lives of those for whom he cares.

"Indeed God speaks once, Or twice, yet no one notices it. In a dream, a vision of the night, When sound sleep falls on men, While they slumber in their beds, Then He opens the ears of men, And seals their instruction, That He may turn man aside from his conduct, And keep man from pride; He keeps back his soul from the pit, And his life from passing over into Sheol" (Job 33:14–18).

Tractor Dream

A woman who was often overwhelmed with feelings of remorse and despair came to us for prayer ministry. As we talked, she thought these feelings were the result of postpartum depression and some small complications soon after she delivered her baby. God had blessed her with a beautiful, healthy, and happy baby boy, but even his ever-present smiles were not enough to cheer her. She had always been a happy person—optimistic and outgoing—but now all was gloom and sadness.

Our first counseling session did not reveal any root causes. At the beginning of our second appointment, after we prayed together, we asked her if she had had any dreams since our last meeting. She replied that she had, and related it to us.

"I was riding on a tractor with my grandfather. I was sitting on his knee. As we came to the end of the field, he proceeded to make a very sharp turn while at the same time trying to avoid hitting another tractor nearby. As we made the turn, the cab of the tractor started to break and glass fell around us. I managed to jump clear but the glass cut my grandfather."

As she finished telling the dream, I (Steve) felt that I understood the root of her problem and asked her some questions. Some of her parentage, in particular the branch of her family that was farmers, had been involved in Freemasonry, an occult society. The more recent of these family members were trying to extricate themselves from the group (the sharp turn) without understanding the ramifications and potential for harm (broken glass) if they did not follow proper procedure, such as having prayers of confession and renunciation. As a result, they and their offspring were accountable for the very serious vows they made during initiation and advancement through that organization. We are accountable for the vows we make.

> "If a man makes a vow to the LORD, or takes an oath to bind himself with a binding obligation, he shall not violate his word; he shall do according to all that proceeds out of his mouth" (Numbers 30:2).

The problems she had been experiencing were rooted in the generational sins of those who had been associated with Freemasonry. We proceeded to pray through them, setting her free to enjoy life again. God expressed his love in giving her that information in a dream. Apart from God's message in that dream, how would we have known where to look?

Be alert to the role of a father-in-law or grandparents from the spouse's side of the family in dreams. They may indicate a generational issue that comes to you through your spouse, which can influence you as well. In each of these cases, you are not to blame the person in the dream, but to see in his or her role an indication of a problem that exists in your life. The issue is not in finding fault, but in finding the solution and healing.

Buildings or Rooms

Houses can often represent our lives. In our dreams, we often recognize the homes as ours, but sometimes there is a twist. The house in a dream may be significant in identifying some point in the dreamer's life. This is important in understanding the message of the dream and is often an indicator about a problem stemming from that time in her life.

Childhood Home

In a dream, someone asked the dreamer's help to remove a tree stump with its roots. When the dreamer arrived at the location, he recognized that it was the neighborhood of his youth. The tree stump that he was to remove was beside the driveway of the house where he grew up.

The message of this dream pointed to a root issue from his youth that he needed to address and give to the Father for permanent removal.

The Shed

A man dreamed of cleaning the shed at the back of the house where he grew up. A shed is a place where we store things we like to keep out of sight, often so that the rest of the property looks nice and neat. As he cleaned the shed, a huge spider crawled out and left. Are there areas of our lives that could use that kind of cleaning? Are there things "out of sight" that are affecting our relationship with others?

Closets, Basements, and Attics

Similarly, closets, basements, and attics often represent places where we hide things, hoping to forget them. However, trying to forget the past is not the solution, because those experiences eventually leak the negative emotions or trauma associated with them, affecting current situations. At some point, if we want freedom, we need to acknowledge these hidden problems and present them to the Father for a thorough cleaning.

The Way of the Closet

A woman dreamed of having to climb through her parent's closet in order to enter the room of a friend with whom she was having difficulties. God was drawing her attention to some problems related to either her parents or ancestors as the cause of her present difficulties in relationships. This does not indicate that her parents caused her problems. It is more likely related to some hidden situation or response to her parents.

We need always to be careful not to blame others for our difficulties. Throughout our lives, people will on occasion hurt us emotionally or physically. We need to guard how we respond to them,[76] because God holds us accountable for our response.

Wet Floor

"I watched a young couple buying a house. They went through the house and were ready to buy it because they liked it. I found myself in the recreation room and noticed that the carpet was soggy and wet because it had started to rain outside. I drew the attention of the real estate agent to the floor, stating that if it were not for the rain, we would not have seen this problem before buying the house. It would have been a costly repair. He said there was a clause in the contract that would cover this problem."

In this dream, the rain represented hardships that we sometimes experience. Hardships can be good, as it is through them that we often learn things about ourselves, things that may otherwise go unnoticed. As Paul declared, "All things work together for good . . . (Romans 8:28). When God resolved the issue, the dreamer had greater ability to experience the joy and peace that God has for us.

Toilets, Baths, and Showers

It's always amusing to listen to people as they tell a dream in which they were in a shower or sitting on a toilet. In most cases the dreams are helpful, representing the cleansing work of the Holy Spirit in our lives. The Old and New Testaments both talk often about the need for washing or cleansing, either as part of a ceremony or as representing the process of sanctification.

As with every dream, we must not let symbols distract us from our priority of unraveling the message of the dream. Toilets represent a subconscious or deeper work of cleansing than a shower or bath. For example, a personality or relationship problem that is hidden in childhood or in our ancestry would require a deeper cleansing than would a habit or sin we have picked up more recently. Dreams may portray the latter as a need for a shower or bath. The following dream has both a toilet and a child and offers interesting insight into a barrier to healing.

Busy Washroom

"I was at a party, looking for the washroom. Someone directed me upstairs and when I found the washroom, a four or five-year-old little girl was playing there. She would not leave to allow me to use it, so I went to the next stall. When I went in, I realized she had followed me. I led her out and locked the door but she started to push the door in. I fixed the door, told her not to do it again, but she persisted, and again pushed it in. Eventually I took her downstairs to find her parents, but I learned that they had left or abandoned her."

Years of counseling had made little progress in relieving this woman of the emotional pain she carried—a fact the dream had made clear by her inability to use the toilet. The key in this dream was that God was revealing the reason for the lack of progress. A dissociate memory (the little girl) wanted and needed attention. Until the woman and her counselor addressed that issue, it would continue to interrupt (push at the door), preventing the inner healing. During prayer ministry, that information would be literally, and actually, a Godsend!

Actions in Dreams

A man shared a recurring dream in which he always seemed to be late for appointments—something always interfered and prevented him from reaching his destination. In each dream the plane, car, or train broke down. Sometimes a late arrival or early departure caused him to miss connections.

We have listened to others tell of their frustrations in not being able to find their offices, classrooms, or workplaces. Some wander the halls looking in vain for a room or exit. Others are unable to locate their cars or their homes, and others, no matter how hard they try, are not able to move fast or escape a pursuer. How should we understand such occurrences? If they represent a recurring theme, they may carry an important message for the dreamer.

Always keep in mind that these actions are symbolic and our goal is to understand what they might represent. Ask yourself these questions: "When this activity happens in a dream, what are my feelings? How do I react emotionally?" Make a note of this as well as any you would feel if that scenario took place in your real life. One man, whose dreams had recurring themes along these lines, noted the following:

- I get frustrated.

- I get angry.
- I feel helpless.
- I feel out of control.

As we talked about these feelings and compared them to his personality and his demeanor at work, we concluded that he was happiest in life when he was in control. Lack of control brought on frustration and anger. Once we established this, we understood that God was trying to make him aware of control issues in his life and that this was not necessarily a desirable trait.

As long as he tried to control events in his life, God would not be able to work on his behalf.[77] Trusting God and wanting to control everything were in direct conflict with each other. Which did he want operating in his life? Either he surrendered control to God and allowed him to guide his life, or he maintained control and took responsibility for the consequences.

This, for him, was a sanctification issue. It was clear to us where God was leading him, but he had to come to that conclusion on his own. He eventually repented of his obsession with control, asking God to remove it from his life and choosing to trust the Father to guide and direct him. Subsequently, his loved ones noticed a marked change in him.

Some other actions or activities in dreams to which we should give attention:
- gangsters
- not being able to locate things
- misplacing things
- climbing things

Sexual Dreams

Symbols relating to sex, including intercourse can appear in our dreams. Christians are often repulsed at the thought that they would have sexual dreams, however, with the exception of "incubus"[78] and "succubus"[79] dreams, they are quite acceptable. We must remember to look for the meaning of the symbols, and not inordinately focus on any caressing or sexual acts. They can symbolize union or intimacy, or represent a need to become one with the attributes of the other person in the dream, assuming the dreamer knows him or her. If the other person is unfamiliar, a sexual dream may represent a warning of a wrong union or a change of attitude toward the person with whom you are intimate. This warning is not to condemn, but to draw your attention to a change that may be creeping in.

Cheating Dream

A woman shared this story with me.

"I have been in a relationship for just over a year and during that time, I have experienced several dreams that I am becoming worried about. Initially I would have dreams about kissing another man who would be either someone I previously had a crush on or had not seen in a long time. I have had dreams like this before, so I was not that worried.

"Eventually it progressed to men who were currently in my life—friends or coworkers. In these dreams, I was fully aware that I was cheating and that it was wrong. Once I dreamt about a man that I used to go to school with. It was very explicit, and even though we did not have sex, I knew I was cheating, but I didn't care."

After hearing this, I (Steve) asked the woman two questions:

"Have you at any time made a commitment to the Lord? Is it possible that you have been cheating on that commitment?"

After a few moments of silence, she replied that my questions spoke to her. Our conversation ended on that note. She obviously had discovered some things to think about and respond to in prayer.

Intimate Qualities Dream

One man shared that the message he received from a sexual dream was that he needed to become one with, or assimilate the skills represented by the people he was being intimate with in the dream. Subsequently he began to acquire the relevant organizational and business skills that prepared him for a new ministry.

Nakedness in Dreams

Many people tell of being naked in dreams. Some dreamers are concerned about this in the dream; others are not. Usually nakedness is simply symbolic of being open and having nothing to hide, and as such it is a good symbol. It is the opposite of hypocrisy, which has its origin in hiding behind a mask.

Conclusion

Whether the symbols in your dream are sexual or they involve people, relatives, or children, do not allow the symbols to distract you from looking for the message of the dream. Understanding the message is the goal—the objective. We are always trying to answer the question: "What is God trying to say to us in our dreams?"

We have looked at only a few symbols that may represent a healing message. To try to document and explain every possible symbol would have us competing with God's creativity. Instead, we hope these examples will help you find ways to view dream symbols in increasingly abstract ways. Let them teach you to become a lateral thinker, a thinker that steps back to ask the question, "In what other way or angle can I view this symbol that will be different from how I normally see it?" Pray for and expect guidance. Through it all, we hope that the process of applying those symbols to dreams and inner healing will be a rewarding one.

11 Dreams and Inner Healing

For God does speak—now one-way, now another-though man may not perceive it. In a dream, in a vision of the night, when deep sleep falls on men as they slumber in their beds, he may speak in their ears and terrify them with warnings, to turn man from wrongdoing and keep him from pride, to preserve his soul from the pit, his life from perishing by the sword (Job 33:14–18 NIV).

As we have said, the process of sanctification is a cooperative or interactive one. God shows us what area of our life he wants to sanctify, but we have to choose to bring it to him to do the work. If we try to sanctify ourselves, we soon find ourselves under the law or legalism and we inevitably fall deeper into sin. Paul tells us the power of sin is the law[80] and that we should present our bodies as a living sacrifice.[81] God does not drag us onto the operating table so that he can do the sanctifying. Rather he waits until we decide of our free will that we need the operation and voluntarily climb onto the table. At each stage of the sanctification process, we must choose to be involved.

When we are aware of sin in our lives, we can confess it and ask the Father to remove it. However, it becomes a little more difficult when confronted with events and actions that we have tried to hide, bury, and forget—things that took place years or even decades ago. Maybe we do not even remember them, so we do not know what to bring to the Father. How can we become aware of these issues so that we can resolve them?

"In a dream, in a vision of the night," he is able to reveal not only the future but also the past, the things forgotten, events we may have been too young to remember, sins committed by our predecessors about which we were never aware. He is able to reveal hidden issues so that they can be healed, but are we able to understand them?

Healing dreams

TV Programming

"I (Steve) dreamt I was in a bed with a friend and beside me was a large TV. I turned it on and played with the controls. By accident, I found a secret list of options in a hidden menu. I selected the first option, which, as I watched, seemed to be some programmer's personal images. These images seemed tasteful at first but became pornographic. Initially I was glad my friend was behind me and could not see what I was watching, but eventually the images embarrassed me and I looked for ways to return to the main menu. Finally, when there seemed to be no way to stop the images, I switched the TV off."

This was a personal dream—for and about me. In my dream language, I know the person in bed with me in the dream was Jesus, representing an intimate relationship.

Years ago, I had a problem with pornography that I thought I had overcome. In this dream, God was showing me that I still had a hidden attraction in this area. I needed to know this so I could continue to bring it before God in prayer, seeking continuing sanctification. If I did not get help, that sin could reaffirm its hold over me.

The dream was not condemning, but rather an expression of God's love for me.

If God had not given me the dream, I would have remained deceived that I was free of that problem. Carelessness or over confidence combined with my sinful nature could easily have drawn me back into sin.

The Frog

"I (Steve) was in a spaceship, looking through a round window at the earth far below. I pointed toward Europe, showing the captain, a woman, where I was born. As I pointed, the moon passed between us, blocking the view. We moved the ship to a different location so we could still see earth.

"It was time to eat and I walked to a table of food where I saw one plate with a grotesque, half-eaten frog on it. I was going to take a different dish when the captain told me to take the frog, so I did. As I was walking away from the table, I picked the frog up off the plate and as I did, it peed onto my foot."

As I woke from this dream, I understood its meaning and intent. I was born in the Netherlands and that dream caused me to remember a story my parents told of events during World War II. It concerned the liberation of our area by the Allies—in this case they were French soldiers. Apparently these soldiers had head lice and other hygienic problems.

While listening to those stories as a child (passing moon), I concluded that all French people were dirty (grotesque frog). While growing up, I had often been exposed to the slanderous term 'frog" as referring to people of French descent. Over time, I hid this prejudice in my heart. It eventually started unconsciously affecting my Christian walk (peeing on my foot). This attitude was not Christ-like! The Holy Spirit (captain) used the dream to make me aware of my prejudice against the French and I was then able to confess it and ask the Father to remove it from my life. This brought me another step closer to being like Jesus. Soon after this dream, I entered into business dealings with a French Christian businessman. Just a coincidence?

The Bathroom Stall

A woman told us this dream. It had many symbols related to hidden issues for inner healing.

"I was in a motel room with my husband and my young daughter (my children are all grown). The government had ordered everyone to surrender their belongings and climb into trucks. The three of us escaped from the trucks.

"Then I was hiding under a blanket on a front lawn. Other people were around me, but they were only hunting for me. The man I feared kept walking into the area where I was hiding. I tried to go into the backyard to hide, but this same man was hosting a party there.

"Next, I am in a factory where I am determined to escape. I am making plans to escape and others are trying to help and protect me as I look for a room to hide in. I am looking for an exit out of this place and I know the exits are near bathroom stalls. The dream ends with me trying to escape."

The dream represents a vignette of this woman's life. She was in a temporary place (motel) with her husband (Jesus) and young daughter. At the time of the dream, her children were adults. This young daughter represents a time in her life when she experienced something traumatic, something likely hidden in her subconscious. The three of them escaped the trucks when she became a Christian, and her daughter stayed with her even then.

In the next scene, she is hiding under a covering in the front yard (conscious memory), while the enemy is having a party (creating havoc) in her backyard (unconscious memory). In the last scene, she is caught up in the routines of life (the factory) and wants to escape. Somehow, she knows the way out is through an exit beside the bathroom stall, which represents deep cleansing, or inner healing.

We asked her a few questions, looking for indicators that she may have something hidden in her subconscious. She identified a few such as missing memories, frequently misplaced items, and unexplainable mood swings. Each of these is a strong indicator of hidden trauma and possibly dissociated memories.

School Yard

"In this dream, my wife and I were holding hands as we walked away from a school. I told her to act naturally so we would not draw anyone's attention. I had killed my son and left him in a fetal position in the schoolyard."

This is an awful dream for any parent to wake up from, especially if we forget that as a personal dream, the people in them are only symbols, they do not represent the real people in our lives. Here too, the son was younger in the dream than in real life. This is often an indictor, as it was in this dream, that he represents an issue from the dreamer's past. Intimacy (holding hands with his wife), training (school), and allowing the training to work out in the dreamer's life (schoolyard) had ended the negative affects of an earlier buried memory of the dreamer. It was in the schoolyard that others had bullied, demeaned, and isolated him. That issue was now dead.

The Operation

"I was lying on something resembling an operating table, but did not know why I was there. A man was pressing down hard on my left leg, causing pain. Then I started to notice a growing pain in my right leg. I realized that the man was causing the pain in my left leg to divert my attention from my right leg. I got up to look at my right leg. Someone had cut it from the outside of my kneecap up to my hipbone. It was a very deep, clean cut and at a slight angle.

"Someone had pulled the upper part of the flesh to the side, as if they wanted to get a better look underneath. There was no blood, no veins, just a big hunk of flesh. The wound was in the shape of a triangle, with the tip of the triangle pointing to the knee. I realized they had taken out a growth the size of a large coin from the area of my hipbone. I did not understand why they needed to make such a large incision. I wondered if there would be a permanent scar on my leg. Why didn't they just make a small incision?"

The dreamer was the son of missionaries and had lived most of his life in three countries. He had been experiencing much emotional pain, as he had to live in a country that he did not consider to be "home." He came asking for

Dreams and Inner Healing

help in understanding this dream.

Prior to the dream, he had visited the country he considered his home while on vacation. When it came time to leave, he was overwhelmed with grief. Through this dream, God was showing the man that his present emotional pain was a ruse (the pressure on his left leg) and that the real problem was deeper (the deep incisions on his right leg and thigh). The problem was beneath the triangle, the three countries in which he and his family lived as missionaries.

As a boy, he had attended boarding schools and was separated from his parents for long periods of time, followed by short visits with them. After each visit home, he would face the emotional pain of leaving those he loved and needed. When the recent vacation ended, the emotion of these childhood memories returned, causing him months of grief and depression.

God wanted this man to know that his problems had deep roots and that only God could heal them. After this dream the superficial symptoms no longer fooled the man. He became determined to take the root issues to Jesus, the Wonderful Counselor, and be free of them.

The Racetrack

"We were running on a racetrack. Each time I had to choose the outer lane, which was winding and seemed a difficult path and said "HEALING" on the top. I was exhausted and wanted to lie down for the night on the narrow strip of rock. I could only sleep on one side, facing one direction. If I turned, I would fall down the precipice to my death. In my mind, I pondered that it seemed easier to just give up and die. I prayed 'Lord, protect me when I sleep, that I don't turn over.' I was too tired and fell asleep."

The first part of this dream informed the dreamer of her present situation. Her life seemed difficult, as if she was always on the outer path (she was on a track that was winding and difficult, a path on the outer lane). However, there was an assurance that healing is imminent (the path was marked for HEALING). She was tired and wanted to rest (exhausted and felt the desire to lie down), but even rest seemed difficult to achieve (a narrow strip of rock). She also felt that if she made even an unconscious (sleep) choice to turn in another direction, that there would be danger (she would fall to her death).

This dreamer was at the end of her rope (it seems easier just to give up and die), but the Lord was letting her know that even in the midst of the difficult time of healing, she was able to reach out to him (the prayer she prayed in the dream). With that, she was peaceful enough to fall asleep. The dream indicated that the dreamer was on a healing journey and although it was difficult, she was still reaching out to the Lord.

Swimming the River

"I had instructors teaching me how to swim in the river and sustain myself in the water without drowning. I followed their instructions and was able to reach the deep part of the river. I thought I was drowning, but with one leg I made movements that kept me afloat. I was impressed. The instructors called me back to the shore. I was so excited that I could sustain myself in the water and I told them, 'These past 10 years I have tried and I could never do this.' They encouraged me and said I was getting ready for another assignment."

Instructors (Jesus, the Holy Spirit, and the Father) are now teaching this dreamer some important things. The river

Dreams and Inner Healing

can represent a place of refreshment, healing, and future ministry. The instructors are teaching the dreamer how to sustain herself without drowning. God is enabling her to go deeper into the things he has for her (the deeper part of the river) and she will be sustained in that place with no fear of death (drowning). She is called back to the Lord (her instructors) to learn an important lesson.

For 10 years, she has tried to accomplish things in her own strength but not been successful (I could never do this). Now, with the instruction of the Lord, she is encouraged by what she is able to accomplish. Perhaps, with her season of healing now over, she is ready for another assignment.

Snake's Tongue

"I saw a snake going away from me. What drew my attention was its tongue."

This dreamer described the context of her life. The previous night others had prayed for her healing, and this included generational or ancestral issues. She understood the dream to mean she had received healing of the tongue (her problem with gossiping). The dream indicates that as the healing takes place, the snake will leave the dreamer.

Mother in the River

"My mother was floating in the river. She was very sick. At some point, she turned into my sister, who was also in the river. My sister then started to take on the characteristics of my mother."

The dreamer noted that in the two following nights her dreams had the same theme. This is an impersonal dream. The river represents the flow of generational history of her family. The mother who is in the river is very sick and there is a need for healing. The mother turns to her sister. The characteristics of the mother that are becoming evident in the sister are what the Lord wants the dreamer to pray about in intercession for her sister.

Green Park

"I was walking through a big green park early in the morning. It was so peaceful. I started walking up a high hill. At the top, I found a way out of the park. I noticed that there was a bear behind some hedges, sleeping on his back with his feet in the air. As I came closer and tried to pass him, he awoke. I ran back down the hill and through the park into a day care center.

"I hid there, but I still heard the bear moving around, looking for me. I went into another room. As I was looking for the door, I saw some cases of soda and had the idea to pour some on the floor so the bear would drink it. Then I heard the bear coming in the other door, so I started running down the hall to tell others not to go into the room where the bear was. Then a man said that I should have told him not to open that door because he had already let the children in."

Even though it was a seemingly peaceful time in the dreamer's life (big green park), this person came upon a bear. There is an issue in this person's life for healing that was not yet awakened to the conscious level (the bear is sleeping), but now the problem has come to life (the bear awakens). The issue was pursuing the dreamer, and no matter what he did, it followed wherever he ran. The Lord was probably counseling the dreamer to get healing for problems from his childhood (the day care into which he runs), but the issue successfully pursues him and, once again, the dreamer is running. At the end of this dream, a man let the children into the room where the bear was. Running from the problem will not resolve it, facing the bear will.

Dreams and Inner Healing

This dreamer has a problem represented by the bear (we are not so concerned as to what the issues are but only that it represents issues). They are related to childhood (the children in the day care with the bear). The dreamer has locked the problems away since childhood and now the Lord is counseling him to seek healing of them (bear).

Wrong Steps

"I was with Shirley, my daughter-in-law, and five other women. We came to an old, gray, brick building, kind of run down on the outside. Shirley went up seven steps and immediately came down saying, "Wrong steps." Then Shirley and the other women went up the six steps. I decided to go out of the building and go another way. I had to stay close to the building, because someone had dug a ditch around the edges and I was afraid of falling into it.

"When I went around to the back, I found myself in an open field. I realized I was lost there, but then I found the building. I entered and walked through the rooms. In one room a baby in light green pajamas was lying on a large bed, crying. As I approached, it stopped crying. I touched the baby's face and then I left the room."

This dreamer's life (represented by the building) is old, gray, and run down. She has taken "wrong steps." When she decided to go another way in life, she found herself frayed around the edges (dug out edges, like a ditch). Even when her life seemed to open up (field), she was lost. In her life (back in the building again), she discovered there was an area that needed healing.

The Lord was gracious to indicate the period in her life that she should focus on (the baby) and so stop the crying. There is hope in this dream. The baby was wearing green pajamas. Green often represents new life and the pajamas indicate sleep, a time when there should be peace. The dreamer acknowledged the issues for healing (she goes to the baby and touches her face).

Clark Gable

"While with a friend, I was bragging that on two occasions I had visited Clark Gable. I was pleased that he singled me out and invited me to his house. He was respectable and seemed platonically delighted to be in my company. He referred to our times together as 'Moonlight and Roses.'

"My friend and I were driving to his house. I was not sure why, because I wanted to keep Clark's attention to myself and not share it with her. However, on the way there, my friend wanted to stop and make fans out of twigs. She told me that to do this, we would also need soap. I thought the idea was stupid, but did not say so."

The first part of this dream spoke about God's (Clark Gable) attitude toward the dreamer. The dreamer was special (singled out and invited to his house). He was delighted with the dreamer. Their times together were as "moonlight and roses."

The second part showed the attitude of the dreamer that the Lord wanted to heal. She demonstrated an exclusive rather than inclusive attitude toward her friend (I wanted to keep all of his attention to myself and not share it with her). Whatever the friend represented distracted (wanted to stop and make fans) the dreamer from what she really wanted. Even though she resented the delay, she said nothing about it. Perhaps this too represents an issue for healing.

French Décor

"Some woman and I had rented a cottage for a night.

It was beautifully decorated with what I call Country French décor. I kept looking around the bedroom, finding many lovely touches—fancy fluffy feminine spreads and curtains. I had chosen my bed and settled in when about five women entered. They were admiring the room and I finally asked them what they were doing there. They told me they were staying in the room too. I wondered what was going on. They informed me the room was for a group of 14.

"I said, 'Oh my, where will we all shower?' I had not yet found a bathroom. I looked for the shower and I found it behind a curtain in the kitchen. It seemed to make sense to me, because somehow I knew the building was built in the 40's, before bathrooms were common in houses."

An important symbol to focus on in this dream is the number 40 and whatever happened to cause the "cottage" of her life to become crowded. The dreamer was aware that the cottage had been built in the 40's. When she was seven years old (1943), her father had become a serious alcoholic and since that time, she had been the family peacekeeper, especially when the father was on a binge. He would be violent to everyone except her and she often protected her mother. Until she left home when she was 18 years old, her life consisted largely of protecting family members. She had no happy memories of her childhood.

The dream revealed to the dreamer her desire for healing and cleansing (she is concerned about and looks for the shower and bathroom). The dream ends well, encouraging the dreamer to continue with the healing process (she finds the shower).

Hospital Baby

"I was a year-old baby in the hospital. Doctors took

me into a room and put me on a cold metal table. I was naked. Doctors, male and female, took pictures of me, telling me to move so they could get better pictures of me in humiliating positions—my genitalia exposed. I felt ashamed, unworthy, and sad, as no one was there to help me. I woke up depressed."

The year-old baby is a symbol indicating a time period for which healing is required. The dreamer subsequently described the context of his birth as being very difficult. As a young child, he was in poor health, requiring several hospital stays. One hospitalization lasted three weeks before his father removed him because his condition was deteriorating. The dreamer had asthma and bronchitis, perhaps the very things the Lord wanted to heal.

The dream revealed problems related to shame, humiliation, abandonment, unworthiness, depression, and rejection. They all still affected the dreamer. The Lord wanted to heal these areas, all of which are probably rooted in the birth and hospital experiences of the dreamer.

African Savannah

"My friend and I were hunting in the African savannah. I had a rifle and I was looking through the scope. My friend pointed out an impala but I was not interested, thinking there was better game. We walked on and I discovered 11 or 13 black-hooded cobras in a swampy, muddy, area, swinging back and forth and standing about knee high.

We walked on and came to a cave entrance. We were about to enter when I told my friend that I intended to return to the cobras and shoot one, to see what would happen. As we turned, I was startled to see the cobras behind me. They then turned into dark and shadowy scaly-skinned men and

Dreams and Inner Healing

women.

"I pointed my gun at them, slipped a bullet into the chamber, and asked, 'Who are you and what are you doing?' A woman answered me saying, 'We are African pygmies on our way to an island by a tunnel. This cave is the entrance.' I was curious and apprehensive, so I told them to lead me."

This dream had many symbols that were personal to the dreamer. He had lived in Africa for seven years and enjoyed hunting. The scope on the gun symbolized the clarity and focus that the Lord had for him. The cobras symbolized a need for healing of a muddy area in his life. The pygmies were dangerous and God was saying it would be dangerous not to pay attention to problems that needed healing. The cave entrance and tunnel reminded him of the birth canal. The Lord was speaking about the healing required in his early life. This dreamer was excited about finally understanding the roots of some serious problems. With an understanding friend, he took part in healing prayer.

Secondhand Auction

"I was at a secondhand auction with my mom, Fiona, and Tim. I was selling my mom's old electric hot plate, a stack of old towels, and a lot of my wardrobe. I was also selling a metal box with another box that fit inside it. It made a terrible noise when I opened it. I was wondering whether to keep the hot plate for when I moved away from home, but mom and Fiona said I should not because I didn't know when that would be and I could probably get a cheap one then. As well, we never really used the old hot plate because it was too bulky. Therefore, I left it in a pile to sell for $100 so I could travel."

In the context of the dreamer's life, the weekend

before the dream she had been dealing with some problems of rejection and found herself responding in anger. This dream is probably informing her of some generational problems or issues that require healing (second hand things from her mom). Some are "hot" issues (hot plate) in her life. Through healing, the dreamer can lose many of her bad habits she has of relating to others (a lot of her wardrobe).

Even the things she has stored away inside (the box inside the box) are problems affecting her current life, crying out for healing (made a terrible noise when opened). This dreamer was about to move out of the old and into a new future (discussion of moving out from home, leaving the old hot plate and getting a new one later). As the Lord redeems the old ($100), this dreamer will move on to new experiences in life (travel).

Mountain Desert

"I was in a desert place in the mountains. There were two men, each bringing a sack of money to me. They could not see each other, but were calling to each other and to me about the place where we would meet. I was concerned about this, because there were bandits about and they too would hear about the meeting place. Then I was with one of the men. I saw his gun and asked for it because I wanted to protect what was mine."

The dreamer and his boss work in one division of a company. The boss is sickly, often sleeping on the job and doing little work. But when he presents projects or ideas to his superiors, the boss takes credit for things the dreamer has done. For several weeks the dreamer had been thinking of asking for a promotion. He would not say anything to dishonor his boss, but he felt that maybe it was time to progress more. This dream came a few weeks after he had been pray-

Dreams and Inner Healing

ing for direction.

In the dream, the money signified abundant blessings the Lord wanted to bring him. There was a double portion for him. When asked what the men represent to him, the dreamer answered that he was really only aware of one man and he knew this man as being faithful. There was a concern in the dream that someone could steal what was his—the boss was that thief. The dreamer's faithfulness (the man representing faithfulness) is what is bringing the Lord's blessing and prosperity (the money) to him. He is determined to protect what was his (taking of the gun) with authority. Overall, this dream encouraged the dreamer to reach out for the blessings of the Lord by applying for the promotion.

Conclusion

Having helped hundreds of people interpret their dreams, we have regularly been surprised to see how many times the Lord brings to mind past issues that prevent us from enjoying the freedom that Jesus promises us. With more perseverance and diligence than any parent, God our Father works to set us free of things that ail us. His ability to reveal hidden influences that hinder us in this life is nothing short of marvelous.

These dreams do not represent condemnation, nor do they affect our salvation, since there is no condemnation for those in Christ, and our salvation is sure.[82] These dreams represent issues in our lives through which we have given the enemy legal access to rob us of a life full of joy, peace, and love. Removing these problems denies the enemy access, allowing us to grow spiritually. We give them legal access when we willfully disobey God's word.[83]

Be attentive to the messages God delivers to you

through dreams. Be quick and ready to respond to their messages by surrendering necessary areas of your life to God. And always remember that the only reason we can expect any healing at all is because of the work Jesus completed on the cross.

12 The Scary Dreams of Children

But Jesus said, "Let the children come to me. Don't stop them! For the Kingdom of Heaven belongs to such as these" (Matthew 19:14, NLT).

Has any parent not experienced the travail of a child awakened by a scary dream? And what of the frustration of not being able to help them? Many parents inevitably wonder if the dreams are just the product of "random neuron firing" of a busy mind or if God is giving dreams that frighten them. Could there be an important message hidden among those scary images?

In our efforts to understand the dreams of children, there are important factors to consider. Young children often cry easily, with the least provocation. A playmate takes a toy and a child's screams imply a calamity has occurred. Be mindful of this point when you console them.

Avoid overused reassurances such as "It was only a dream," or, "You're awake now, it was just a dream." These comments imply that dreams are not important. Instead, try to get the child to talk about the dream, not only in an effort to calm him down but also to get an idea of what the dream was about. There may be an important message—for you!

In our experience of helping interpret the dreams of children, we have learned that the Lord gives them for many reasons. Children often see Jesus and angels in their dreams and Jesus uses dreams to play with children and encourage them, so that they know he knows what is going on in their lives and that they are important to him.

In this chapter, we focus on what we call caregiver's dreams, a caregiver being the parent or guardian who has the primary responsibility for the child.

The Caregiver's Dream

While most dreams are personal dreams, a child's personal dream is different in that the message of the dream might not be for the child, but for the caregiver (parent or guardian). The child's dream is about the child, but it is given in order to draw a response from the child's caregiver(s). Because of this, it is important that caregivers pay attention to the dreams of children who are below the age of accountability.[84] These children are usually powerless to affect change in their situations. Through a child's dream, God may be drawing the caregivers' attention to a child's problem.

Daycare Dilemma

Through his tears, a young boy related a dream of three big people with mean-looking faces chasing him. He was frightened. Regardless of how hard he tried, he could not get away from them. This dream was similar to others that the boy had experienced over a period of weeks and is an example of a caregiver's dream.

The Scary Dreams of Children

Soon afterwards, the boy's father picked him up from his daycare center a little earlier than usual. As he walked in, he could hear the loud voices of some staff members who were involved in an intense argument. They stopped when they saw the father and quickly adopted a more pleasant demeanor. As he drove home the father remembered the dream and realized that there were three staff members at the daycare center. The dream became clear.

This daycare center, with the angry staff, was the object of the child's dream. When the parents placed their son in another facility with a more pleasant atmosphere, their son's dream stopped. Through the dream, God had caught the parents' attention and they responded by resolving the problem.

Bloody Mary

"In my house was a closet. If someone said 'click' while walking past, the door would open and then slam shut. Bloody Mary lived in that closet. Some people moved in upstairs. They had a pet that went into the closet. The owner went to the closet to get the pet. There was a hole in the wall covered by a cobweb. They pulled on the cobweb. They found a picture of Bloody Mary carving a pumpkin. As they pulled on the cobweb, Bloody Mary pulled them in."

This dream was very frightening to the seven-year-old girl. At that age, she would have had little understanding of the dream. Asking the child about the dream within the context of her life revealed some important problems to the parents. During a sleepover, some children in this girl's Brownie troop told scary stories. A favorite character in many of these stories was Bloody Mary. At that young age, sensitive children have difficulty separating reality from fiction. The stories affected the child for weeks through her

Did God give the dream to the child for her sake, or for the parents? A child would have little or no ability to control the activities at a sleepover. Peer pressure would hold sway. Once alerted to these story times because of the dream, the parents intervened to eliminate future trauma and to counsel their daughter.

The Mud Girl

"My dad and I were lying on a couch. I asked him if I could get some tomatoes for supper. He said yes. I went outside to get them. The mud girl was there but went into the house. She killed my dad. The mud girl told me to go to another place. I just stood there. She told me again but I just stood there. She killed me. I went to heaven and asked Jesus what I should do to the mud girl—should I kill her, or leave her alone? He told me to destroy her. He gave me vinegar. I went and poured it on her and she died. My dad came alive and we had supper."

The little girl who recounted this dream lives in a foster home. Her real parents have separated and her father is in depression, spending most of his time in bed. A part of her believes she was responsible for the difficulties between her parents and for the pain that her father carries. As a child, she is helpless to intervene or to solve the dilemma. Compounding her problem is the foster home situation. Her guardians are limited in their ability to respond to the message of the dream.

Ideally, her parents should hear the dream and understand that she is carrying the responsibility for their separation. They could then correct that misunderstanding and relieve the child of a load she should not have to carry. The caregivers could also seek help for the child.

Snakes

A three-year-old boy woke up and was standing at the side of his crib, crying. After his parents were able to comfort him, he told them he dreamed there were snakes crawling all over him while he lay there. They realized that the older brothers had been catching snakes in the fields around the house and may have been chasing, scaring, or threatening the child with them. After the dream alerted them, the parents were able to stop the snake-catching and help the child cope with his fears.

Ice Cream

"I had to eat chocolate and vanilla ice cream. I knew the chocolate ice cream was bad but the vanilla was good."

Because of family difficulties, social services placed the child who had this dream into the care of a guardian, who unfortunately had little regard for dreams. The child began expressing difficulties through aggressive behavior and a refusal to go to school. The guardian took the child to a counselor who, after listening to an account of the dream and learning a little about the child's background, discerned the message.

The biological mother, who was white, had loved and cared for the child until she died prematurely. Her father, who was black, had abandoned her at birth. The child was responding, in anger and aggression, because of her father's rejection—the chocolate ice cream. As a child, she was not able to respond to the dream, but God gave the dream to alert her caregivers to the root of her anger.

Conclusion

Some may consider the frightening dreams that children have to be nightmares, simply because they are scary.

However, as with an adult's dream, we need to focus on the message behind the symbolism. Too often we discount scary dreams, believing wrongly that they are not from God. Our experience has been that many such dreams carry important messages, when we take time to try and interpret them.

Why would God not give these dreams to the caregivers? We find that the urgency and importance of the issue is much more dramatic as it is experienced by the child. Too often adults would simply pass it off as a bad dream, giving it no attention.

Children are special to the Lord. Today's kids face many problems not experienced by their parents. Relationship conflicts and abuses may be difficult for the child to comprehend and verbalize. Threats might cause them to be secretive. A dream can override these obstacles, alerting the caregivers. If you are a caregiver, pay attention to the dreams of your children.

13   Responding to Dreams

> Therefore everyone who hears these words of Mine and acts on them, may be compared to a wise man who built his house on the rock (Matthew 7:24).

Everyone who acts on his words is on solid ground! This short qualifying phrase holds a key to all we could ever wish to experience in the Christian life. God does not communicate with us through dreams because it is in vogue or a cute thing to do. He has reasons and purposes for doing so, and these relate to our good.[85] Sometimes he wants to encourage us and express his love to us. Other times, he may want to counsel or heal us.

I once had a toy car. The instructions were simple: Press "F" for Forward. Press "R" for Reverse. Would that the "instructions" for interpreting dreams was that simple! It's much more complicated, though, because there are so many choices. Each human is unique. Our life experiences are unique. This alone makes any formulaic method of responding to a dream very difficult when we do not know the message of the dream.

However, once we understand the message of the dream, we usually also know what response is expected of us. Being determined to go through with that expected response is the next small hurdle we face. Knowing that God is good and that he wants goodness and mercy to overtake us should be sufficient motivation.

Our Own Dreams

Since the majority of our significant dreams are personal, we will face this situation most often. As we grow in our understanding of dreams and develop our dream vocabulary, we will frequently identify issues in the message of the dream that demand counsel, sanctification, or inner healing. How do we respond?

Dianne had a dream in which we were ministering to a client. After we finished, she noticed a crack in the hall of our house. This dream had a message and it seemed important. Being a personal dream, our focus was on Dianne and the context of her life. The dream told her that problems that appeared in the client's life had made her look for similar issues in her life. However, Dianne did not have these problems, but the fear was that she might create them. This dream was a warning of things that could happen. Dianne saw that she should leave the client's issues with the client.

This is a simple example. How we respond depends a lot on the complexity of the issue and the services available to us. When we have a "sliver," as in Dianne's case, we can usually remove it ourselves. When the issue is more serious, we should seek help of someone experienced in interpreting dreams. Seeking help can sometimes be the best response to a dream.

Responding to Dreams

We must remember that we were saved and placed into a community—the body of Christ. In that body, God has given different spiritual gifts. No one is self-sufficient. We are interdependent, in relationship, and ministering to each other's needs.

> "Is anyone among you sick? Then he must call for the elders of the church, and they are to pray over him, anointing him with oil in the name of the Lord; and the prayer offered in faith will restore the one who is sick, and the Lord will raise him up, and if he has committed sins, they will be forgiven him. Therefore, confess your sins to one another, and pray for one another, so that you may be healed. The effective prayer of a righteous man can accomplish much" (James 5:14–16).

Call the elders; confess to one another. These phrases imply community, not isolation. Even the Lord's Prayer starts with "Our Father," not my Father. God designed us so that we need each other. When our dreams speak to us of deeper issues that require inner healing, we should seek out those who are gifted or have authority to help us.

When We Need Help

As discussed throughout this book, we may encounter symbols in our dreams that relate to problems rooted deep in our past. Some may go back to our predecessors, representing "sins of the fathers." They may involve abuses, or the dreamers may see images and symbols for which they have no conscious knowledge. In these situations, dreamers should seek the help of someone qualified who can help you find answers, or resolve the problems.

Some of our clients had suspicious images in their dreams that seemed to be the result of previous dabbling in the occult. Others with similar dreams had been the victims of ritual abuse. The latter required the assistance of someone experienced in this type of ministry.

If, while responding to a dream in prayer, either alone or with a friend, you find that things are getting too intense or more than you can handle, pray a simple prayer asking Jesus to close it down and seal it. Then arrange for more experienced help.

We believe God gives us dreams for a purpose. If we choose to do nothing, and the dream relates to an issue of sin in our lives, we will experience the consequences of continuing in that sin. If the dream relates to an area of hurt and we do nothing, then we will continue to live in the bondage of those wounds.

> "It was for freedom that Christ set us free; therefore keep standing firm and do not be subject again to a yoke of slavery" (Galatians 5:1).

Pursue freedom! Especially freedom from spiritual and emotional wounds that imprison and rob us of life, joy, and peace during our time on earth.

The Dreams of Others

As we grow in our awareness of dreams and dream language, we may develop insights into the dreams of others. This could suggest a gifting in dream interpretation, or just that we have an awareness that enables us to help others understand their dreams.

As we begin to help others, there will be instances when we must use tact and wisdom in describing what we feel the dream may be conveying. It is not always loving and appropriate to tell someone that his dream indicates that he needs deep healing of emotional problems that are rooted in events of the past—events he may not even remember. We

Responding to Dreams

need to be loving, humble, and considerate in our approach to those we hope to help.

If, when others ask our help with their dreams, we see deep-seated problems that are causing harm, direct them to someone competent who can help them. A pastor may be a first good choice, although some fail to see the difference between soul-based wounds and salvation.

(Soul-based wounds are "soul" problems that have nothing to do with salvation. If the dreamer has accepted Jesus into his or her life, salvation is sure. These soul issues are merely openings, through which the enemy robs the dreamer of an abundant, joyful life. Finding any soul problems and resolving them removes the enemy's access into the dreamer's life.)

If a dreamer asks your help with a dream, remember that you are not responsible for their response to the dream; only the direction you give them. Be wise. Know your limitations.

14 Conclusions

Dianne had this dream.

"A woman and I had been scrapping for a long time. She chased me a lot. Someone told me about an escape so I went down some stairs, opened a narrow door, crawled through, and latched the door behind me.

"The next time I saw that woman she had a wooden gun and I had a wooden rifle. I took her gun from her, but she also had something with which she could hit me. I put my rifle down and said, 'This is enough, no more!' I asked her how long she had been chasing me and she said, 'Years and years.' I replied, 'Enough mental energy and time!' She agreed. Putting her weapon down, we embraced."

Dianne experienced an amazing amount of peace after having this dream. Although she did not identify the conflict, there was resolution to a problem that had obviously been a source of internal conflict for many years. The healing was almost immediate. The internal conflict was now over. She experienced more peace with herself and with

God's plan for her.

When reading the Bible, it becomes evident that God used dreams to communicate messages to people. The messages had a variety of purposes and because the dreamers esteemed dreams, they responded to the messages they believed were from God. As a result, God was able to extend his kingdom both through the preservation of his people in both the Old and New Testaments. It is impressive to see how God used dreams to save the life of his infant son, Jesus.

In this book, we have spent a great deal of time studying scriptures to learn how God used dreams to bring healing and counsel into the lives of those dreamers. We then applied these insights to the symbols in our dreams today.

Contained within this book is a small portion of our first book, *Dream Dreams*. That book develops more fully the ways of understanding dream categories, types, and approaches to symbols. This book focuses on dreams that are for and about the dreamer, otherwise known as personal or subjective dreams and their use in healing and counsel.

When one receives salvation through Jesus Christ and enters the kingdom of God, the sanctification process begins. We all have emotional and spiritual wounds that rob us of life, joy, and peace. These can come from ancestral sources or our life experiences. Most of us are not aware of the roots or origin of those wounds. God uses dreams to draw our attention to hidden problems as well as those we are aware of but refuse to address. The work of Jesus on the cross brings forgiveness, cleansing, and freedom where we confess, repent, and ask him to bring healing.

As we become more aware of the symbols in our dreams, we recognize indicators of healing issues. In

Conclusions

Chapter 10, we explored many of these symbols. These are just a beginning. Don't limit yourself to our list, because God's creativity is more diverse than we are.

Many times, parents ask us about the dreams of their children. God speaks to children in dreams as he wants to make himself known to them. However, he also uses dreams to bring healing and counsel into their lives. Many times children's dreams can alert or motivate the parent or caregiver to act on their behalf. Encourage your children to share their dreams with you. There are several benefits:

- The child will get your personal attention. The one-on-one-time is invaluable
- Your child will learn that dreams are important because you have made them important. He may develop a listening ear to the Father.
- The Father will have your ear and may inform you of problems in your child's life that require attention

Our God is so creative. Who could ever conceive of the idea of a dream in the night whereby he reaches down into our lives to heal, counsel, and love us? He is a God who is committed to redeeming the lost and to love us into wholeness and health. Through dreams, we have seen marriages grow in intimacy; people's attitudes to workplaces improve significantly; relationships healed; and family members becoming more tolerant and merciful.

At the same time that he is a corporate God, saving people into a body, a family, he is a personal God who knows, intimately, every hair on our heads. He draws us close to him every day and night.

Bless you with sweet sleep and sweet dreams as you

experience a greater intimacy with him and with others.

Sweet dreams!

End Notes

[1] Matthew 10:39
[2] Luke 6:38, 2 Corinthians 9:6
[3] Matthew 5:5
[4] Hebrews 13:8, Psalm 55:19
[5] Matthew 1:20
[6] Matthew 2:12
[7] Matthew 2:13
[8] Matthew 2:19-20
[9] Matthew 2:22
[10] In Dream Dreams, we discuss the similarities and differences of dreams and visions. We treat them as being the same.
[11] Acts 10
[12] Acts 2:17
[13] Savary, L., P. Berne, and S.K. Williams, Dreams and Spiritual Growth: A Judeo-Christian Way of Dreamwork, Paulist Press, Mahwah, NJ. 1984, p.39
[14] Genesis 1:28, 2:19
[15] Genesis 1:27
[16] "כבוד" Harris, R. Laird, Archer, Gleason L Jr., and Waltke, Bruce K. The Theological Wordbook of the Old Testament. Moody Press. Chicago Il, 1980.
[17] Genesis 39:4-6

[18] Deuteronomy 18:11.
[19] Proverbs 3: 11,12
[20] Matthew 2:23
[21] 1 Corinthians 14:33
[22] Romans 13:1-2, 1 Peter 2:13-15
[23] Genesis 20
[24] Matthew 2
[25] Matthew 2 - Joseph, Genesis 15 - Abram
[26] Genesis 41 - Pharaoh, 1 Kings 3 - Solomon
[27] Acts 10 - Peter
[28] Romans 8:29, Ephesians 1:4
[29] Matthew 22:37-38
[30] 1 Corinthians 15:52
[31] Ephesians 2:10
[32] Isaiah 64:8
[33] Genesis 2:16-17
[34] 1 Corinthians 15:22,45
[35] Matthew 27:46, Mark 15:34
[36] Matthew 27:26-41, Mark 15, Luke 18, John 19
[37] Ephesians 4:22, Colossians 3:9
[38] 2 Corinthians 4:7
[39] Romans 3:23
[40] Isaiah 59:2
[41] Romans 6:23
[42] 2 Corinthians 5:21
[43] 1 John 1:9
[44] Luke 11:13
[45] John 14:26
[46] Romans 10:10
[47] Isaiah 9:6
[48] Zeilstra, Rev A. , Cornerstone Christian Counselling Centre. Waterloo, ON
[49] Olson, Dave and Linda, Listening Prayer. ©1996
[50] McNutt, Dr. Francis, FL
[51] Sandford, John, Elijah House, Post Falls, ID
[52] Smith, Dr. Edward M. Family Care Ministries. Campbellsville, KY

End Notes

[53] Elijah House Training for the Ministry of Prayer Counseling, Elijah House Inc., Post Falls, ID, Section 1, p. 2
[54] Ephesians 6:1-3
[55] Matthew 7:1-2
[56] Galatians 6:7-8
[57] Romans 2:1
[58] Matthew 18:21-35
[59] Kylstra, Chester and Betsy. Restoring the Foundations, www.phw.org. See also Numbers 14:18
[60] Any belief that runs contrary to the words or character of God
[61] Romans 10:13
[62] Romans 12:2
[63] Ephesians 4:24
[64] Romans 6 and 7
[65] Matthew 22:37-38
[66] Isaiah 9:6
[67] Prayer was meant to be a dialogue with God, not a monologue to Him.
[68] Matthew 7:17-19
[69] Matthew 6:15
[70] ibid
[71] 1 John 1:9
[72] Luke 10:38-42
[73] Merriam-Webster's Collegiate Dictionary, Tenth Edition. Copyright © 2002 by Merriam-Webster, Inc.
[74] Dream Dreams pg. 129
[75] Daniel 9, Jeremiah 14:20
[76] Matthew 5-7
[77] Proverbs 3:5-6, Philippians 4:6
[78] "incubus" noun (pl. incubi) a male demon believed to have sexual intercourse with sleeping women.
[79] "succubus" noun (pl. succubi) a female demon believed to have sexual intercourse with sleeping men.
[80] 1 Corinthians 15:56
[81] Romans 12:1-2
[82] Romans 8:1

[83] Deuteronomy 28:15ff
[84] That age after which children begin to influence their own environment. In Jewish culture, 13 years old.
[85] Romans 8:28

Bibliography

Books on Hearing God

Bydeley, Steve and Dianne Bydeley, *Dream Dreams*. Belleville, ON, Essence Publishing, 2002.

Conner, Kevin J. *Interpreting the Symbols and Types*. Portland OR: City Bible Publishing, 1992.

Deere, Jack. *Surprised by the Voice of God*. Grand Rapids, Michigan: Zondervan Publishing, 1996.

Hamon, Jane. *Dreams and Visions*. California, USA: Regal Books, 2000.

Milligan, Ira L. *Every Dreamer's Handbook*. Shippensburg, PA: Treasure House, Destiny Image Publishers, 2000.

Owen, W. Stuart. *A Dictionary of Bible Symbols*. London England: Grace Publications, 1992.

Riffel, Herman. *Dream Interpretation*. Shippensburg, PA: Destiny Image Publishers, 1993.

Riffel, Herman. *Dreams: Wisdom Within*. Shippensburg, PA: Destiny Image Publishers, 1990.

Ryle, James. *A Dream Come True*. Lake Mary, Florida: Creation House, 1996.

Sanford, John A. *Dreams: God's Forgotten Language*. New

York, NY: HarperCollins Publishers, 1989.
Sandford, John L. and Paula Sandford. *The Elijah Task*. Tulsa, OK: Victory House, Inc., 1977.
Thomas, Benny. *Exploring the World of Dreams*. New Kensington, PA: Whitaker House, 1990.
Virkler, Mark and Patti, *Biblical Research Concerning Dreams and Visions*, Elma, NY, Communion with God Publications.

Books on Inner Healing

Friesen, James G., Ph.D, *UNCOVERING THE MYSTERY OF MPD*: Its Shocking Origins, Its Surprising Cure, Here's Life Publishers, 1991.
Sandford, John L. and Mark Sandford, *Deliverance and Inner Healing*, Grand Rapids, MI, Chosen Books, 1992.
Sandford, John L. and Paula Sandford, *The Transformation of the Inner Man*, Tulsa, OK, Victory House, 1982.
Kylstra, Chester and Betsy Kylstra, *An Integrated Approach to Biblical Healing Ministry*, Tonbirdge, UK, 2003.

Audio Tapes

Bydeley, Steve and Dianne Bydeley, Open the Door to Dreams, Kitchener, ON, Lapstone Ministries, 2002.
Jackson, John Paul. Understanding Dreams & Visions. Fort Worth, Texas: Streams Ministries International, date unknown.
Riffel, Herman. Christian Dream Interpretation. Elma, New York: Communion with God Ministries Publishers, 1992

Lapstone Ministries
a cross-denominational ministry working to draw the Body of Christ into a deeper relationship with God and each other.

Steve and Dianne are the Founders and Directors of Lapstone Ministries

Other Resources Available
Dream Dreams book
Dream Dreams Workbook (companion book for individual study and group study)
Dream Dreams Workbook Teacher's Manual
Open the Door to Dreams Seminar Audio Tape Set
Open the Door to Dreams Seminar Audio CD Set
Marriage Intimacy Booklet and Seminar CD or Cassette Sets

Booking Seminars
For information on our seminars, ordering books, workbooks, audio or video tapes, contact:

    Website: www.lapstoneministries.org
    Email: info@lapstoneministries.org